ONE NATION
Always
UNDER GOD

ALSO BY SENATOR TIM SCOTT

America, a Redemption Story: Choosing Hope, Creating Unity

Opportunity Knocks: How Hard Work, Community, and Business Can Improve Lives and End Poverty

The Friendship Challenge: A Six-Week Guide to True Reconciliation— One Friendship at a Time (with Trey Gowdy)

Unified: How Our Unlikely Friendship Gives Us Hope for a Divided Country (with Trey Gowdy)

ONE NATION *Always* UNDER GOD

Profiles in Christian Courage

SENATOR TIM SCOTT

BROADSIDE BOOKS

Unless otherwise noted, scripture quotations are taken from The Holy Bible, New International Version®, NIV®. Copyright © 1973, 1978, 1984, 2011 by Biblica, Inc.® Used by permission of Zondervan. All rights reserved worldwide. www.Zondervan.com. The "NIV" and "New International Version" are trademarks registered in the United States Patent and Trademark Office by Biblica, Inc.®

Scripture quotations marked ESV are taken from the ESV® Bible (The Holy Bible, English Standard Version®). Copyright © 2001 by Crossway, a publishing ministry of Good News Publishers. Used by permission. All rights reserved.

Scripture quotations marked KJV are taken from the King James Version. Public domain.

Without limiting the exclusive rights of any author, contributor or the publisher of this publication, any unauthorized use of this publication to train generative artificial intelligence (AI) technologies is expressly prohibited. HarperCollins also exercise their rights under Article 4(3) of the Digital Single Market Directive 2019/790 and expressly reserve this publication from the text and data mining exception.

ONE NATION ALWAYS UNDER GOD. Copyright © 2025 by Timothy Scott. All rights reserved. Printed in the United States of America. No part of this book may be used or reproduced in any manner whatsoever without written permission except in the case of brief quotations embodied in critical articles and reviews. For information, address HarperCollins Publishers, 195 Broadway, New York, NY 10007. In Europe, HarperCollins Publishers, Macken House, 39/40 Mayor Street Upper, Dublin 1, D01 C9W8, Ireland.

HarperCollins books may be purchased for educational, business, or sales promotional use. For information, please email the Special Markets Department at SPsales@harpercollins.com.

Broadside Books™ and the Broadside logo are trademarks of HarperCollins Publishers.

FIRST EDITION

Library of Congress Cataloging-in-Publication Data

Names: Scott, Tim, 1965– author
Title: One nation always under God : profiles in Christian courage / Tim Scott.
Description: First edition. | New York : Broadside Books, 2025. | Includes bibliographical references.
Identifiers: LCCN 2025004341 (print) | LCCN 2025004342 (ebook) | ISBN 9780063435865 hardcover | ISBN 9780063435896 ebook
Subjects: LCSH: United States—History—Religious aspects—Christianity | Christian biography—United States | Christianity and culture—United States | National characteristics, American | United States—Biography | LCGFT: Biographies
Classification: LCC E179 .S43 2025 (print) | LCC E179 (ebook) | DDC 277.3092/2—dc23/eng/20250331
LC record available at https://lccn.loc.gov/2025004341
LC ebook record available at https://lccn.loc.gov/2025004342

25 26 27 28 29 LBC 5 4 3 2 1

To the answer to my Proverbs 18:22 prayer, Mindy, my best friend and wife—you are the blessing God bestowed upon me and my daily inspiration. To my incredible mom, Frances Scott, whose strength, sacrifice, and unshakable belief in God shaped the man I am today. Your prayers built the foundation of my faith, and your love has been my greatest gift.

And to the American people—those who welcomed me into their homes, shared their stories, and inspired me beyond belief during my journey across this great nation. Your faith, resilience, and hope for a brighter future remind me that we are, indeed, one nation always under God.

CONTENTS

Introduction: One Nation Under God   1

Part I: Vision

Chapter 1: A More Perfect Union   11

Chapter 2: William Lloyd Garrison: If the Truth Is on Your Side, Stand Firm   17

Chapter 3: Training a Godly Imagination   28

Chapter 4: Fred Fox: Do Your Best Even When No One Knows   38

Chapter 5: Charles and Margaret Kairouz: Echoes into Eternity   50

Chapter 6: Louida Ware: Live in the Light of Resurrection   62

Chapter 7: Horatio Spafford: Faith Isn't About What We Feel but What We Know   69

Part II: Revival

Chapter 8: Samuel Davies: How Gratitude Leads to Revival   83

Chapter 9: Dorothea Dix: Walking through Darkness, Making Your Own Light   97

Chapter 10: Frances Scott: The God of Miracles Acts on Faith   111

Chapter 11: Jim Lovell: "The Spirit of God Moved upon the Face of the Waters"   120

Chapter 12: Joshua Glover: Freedom Must Be Defended 135
Chapter 13: Eddie Rickenbacker: Every Blessing Is Meant to Be Passed On 148

Part III: Stewardship

Chapter 14: Norman Borlaug: All Work Is Stewardship for God 167
Chapter 15: John Baker: There's No True Healing without the Church 177
Chapter 16: George Washington Carver: The Plant Doctor 184
Chapter 17: Francis Scott Key: America's Story Is Still Being Written 194
Chapter 18: Heroes Will Rise in a Crisis 202
Chapter 19: David Green: God Has a Plan for Our Work 211
Chapter 20: Small Decisions, Seismic Shifts 222
Conclusion: New Beginnings 231

Acknowledgments 237
Notes 239

ONE NATION
Always
UNDER GOD

Introduction

ONE NATION UNDER GOD

From the start, I want you to understand that this is not a book about politics. The last thing the world needs from me is another book about politics. This is not an "inside look" into Congress or the Senate halls. Virtually nobody wants to read about the inner workings of committees or the complex web of legislative procedures that often seem disconnected from the lives of U.S. citizens. This is a book of stories.

In these pages, I tell the true stories of the Christian men and women who shaped our great nation. This book profiles some of the greatest heroes from our nation's founding until today. As you read these stories, you will begin to see a common thread, a throughline.

Many of the most influential people in the history of the United States of America were men and women of great faith. The heroes who shaped our nation infused Judeo-Christian principles into the foundations of every major pillar and system in our country. Through faith, these men and women found the courage to dream of a better future and the strength to turn those dreams into reality. Their unwavering belief in divine guidance and their commitment to living out these principles laid the groundwork for a nation built on justice, liberty, and equality.

Why is this book important? Why do I feel compelled to write it at a time when my life is fuller than it has ever been? Our culture has been gradually shifting, just a degree or two off-center, for several years now. As when a cargo ship making a long journey gradually veers off course, these seemingly minor deviations from truth, faith, and biblical principles have led us to a place that would be unrecognizable to the generations who came before us.

In many aspects of our nation, monumental changes have been made in the right direction. The abolition of slavery, the triumph of women's suffrage, and the advancements in civil rights are milestones that mark our progress. There is much to be proud of, and I do not overlook our achievements.

However, I am equally aware of the moral decay that has been corrupting the soul of our nation. While we have made significant strides forward, we have also lost our way in many respects. The erosion of foundational values has brought us to a crossroads, where the very foundations of what made our nation a shining city on a hill are at risk.

This book is my attempt to address these concerns, to call attention to the critical shifts that have occurred, and to remind us of the principles that once guided us. It is a plea for a return to the truths and faith that have long anchored us and a reflection on how we can navigate the path forward with integrity and purpose.

I am a Christian—a follower of Jesus. Though I officially gave my life to Jesus when I was eighteen years old, most of my childhood was viewed through the lens of Sunday morning and Wednesday evening services. My grandmama was on every church committee, in every prayer group and women's circle... you get the picture. Every page in her Bible was filled with highlights, underlines, and notes. She was the backbone of our family. And oh boy, did she pray! To call her a prayer warrior would be entirely accurate.

I have often said that Grandmama never met a stranger. I have more memories than I can count of her befriending and feeding people I had never met before. If she thought a family needed community or was hungry, in her mind, every time she fed them, she was Jesus's hands and feet. Hosting and loving people was her ministry. It never mattered if we had enough food or money; Grandmama would find a way to stretch the meal and share it.

My mama is also a woman who loves God! She has prayed for my brother, Ben, and me every day of our lives. She was a nurse's assistant for fifty years, changing sheets and bedpans. Never once did she complain about the work—quite the opposite. She considered her work to be her ministry. Every bedpan she changed, and every patient, nurse, or doctor she interacted with, was her chance to show the love of Jesus.

I'm painting the picture of these two women of God to show you the environment I grew up in. We were dirt-poor my entire childhood. There were many times when we did not have enough food to eat or the electricity was turned off because Mama could not afford to make the payment. There were a couple of years when Mama, Ben, and I had to share a bed. Yet when I reflect on my childhood, my mind doesn't linger on the lack of resources. Mostly, I remember how loved I felt. I remember sitting beside Grandmama and Mama as they prayed. They believed with every fiber of their being that God was bigger than our circumstances. They were filled with faith that God had a plan for our lives. They believed that our job was to help make God's plan a reality. We had the obligation to work hard and never give up. God would do His part if we did ours.

Grandmama and Mama radiated hope, infusing every day of my childhood with its light. They held an unwavering belief in a better future for my brother and me, for our community, and for our nation. Their hopefulness shaped my worldview, which is why I am constantly optimistic about the future. Even in some of my darkest moments—being robbed, breaking my neck, nearly dying in a car accident, or when our electricity was turned off—thanks to Grandmama and Mama, my hope has remained steadfast. What I didn't understand then but do now is that their hope was anchored in the promises of Jesus. Their hope was anchored in the faith they carried.

So why am I spending so much time telling you about the mighty women of faith in my family? The answer is simple. I honestly don't believe that my mama and grandmama are all that different from the men and women who founded the greatest nation on earth. Like the women in my family, they fought first on their knees in prayer and second with their acts of great sacrifice and unwavering determination. Their prayers and actions laid a foundation of faith, resilience, and hope that continues to guide us today.

The values that formed our nation are the very same values that were poured into my mama and that she poured into my brother, Ben, and me. Yet in popular culture today, these values are not only viewed as antiquated or irrelevant but are openly mocked. Just a few days before I began writing this book, Kansas City Chiefs kicker Harrison Butker was attacked by virtually every major media outlet for espousing his traditional Catholic beliefs. Beliefs that up until five minutes ago were not only common but also widely respected and considered foundational to the moral fabric of our society. This incident is not isolated; it reflects a broader trend where expressing faith-based values often leads to public ridicule and scorn.

Our cultural landscape is undergoing significant changes, marked by a profound shift away from our religious foundations. Principles that once unified us and provided a shared sense of purpose and identity are now often dismissed as outdated or intolerant. This erosion of respect for Judeo-Christian values is not merely a rejection of our past; it poses a deep and imminent threat to our future. It underscores the urgent need for a collective reckoning—a return to the roots that have historically grounded and guided us. Without this, the famous quote often attributed to Alexis de Tocqueville—"America is great because she is good, and if America ceases to be good, America will cease to be great"—will ring true. It is not military power, economic prosperity, or technological advancement alone that ensures greatness, but a shared moral compass and the cultivation of shared virtues.

Our nation was built on the principles of faith, hard work, and a commitment to justice and equality. These values are the cornerstone of our beginnings. Returning to them will heal the divisions and restore a sense of unity and purpose. This is not just about looking back with fondness on a bygone era but about reclaiming the essence of what forged our nation. How did we become a beacon of hope and freedom?

We can't return to our foundational principles if we relegate them to one day of the week. Jesus's teachings aren't just for Sundays. They're meant to transform our entire lives, and that means the work we do the rest of the time. This book highlights the lessons that enable us to incorporate them into our daily lives.

The life of abolitionist William Lloyd Garrison illustrates how to stand up for Christian truth when the whole world seems to oppose it. Christians like eighteenth-century evangelist Samuel Davies reveal the overwhelming power of gratitude to change our national character.

But more than just lessons, these stories tackle questions. Dorothea Dix's life poses the query of how people can regain faith when all the "faithful" in their lives have failed them. For Horatio Spafford, whose family was lost at sea, the problem was how to keep trusting in God in the face of immense suffering.

The wisdom of these American Christians comes down through the ages. They were journalists, soldiers, actors, immigrants, reformers. In every sphere of life, they found that God gave them the tools to succeed and persevere. It is through their examples that we can learn how to create revival in a country that has turned its face away from God. Across their stories comes this lesson: Revival has to start with a vision, which turns into thankfulness, and that thankfulness is then translated into action—stewardship of the resources God has given us. The United States of America was founded on Judeo-Christian principles and the teachings of Jesus. Judeo-Christian values underlie the most powerful economy in the world, our moral framework, and our legal foundation. Our founding documents, institutions, and culture are deeply rooted in these enduring principles.

Throughout the Scriptures, we see a recurring theme: the necessity of adhering to God's principles to sustain and prosper as a community. Proverbs 14:34 reminds us,

"Righteousness exalts a nation, but sin condemns any people." Moreover, 2 Chronicles 7:14 offers a clear prescription for national healing and redemption: "If my people, who are called by my name, will humble themselves and pray and seek my face and turn from their wicked ways, then I will hear from heaven, and I will forgive their sin and will heal their land." Is it really this simple? Yes!

Throughout this book, I aim to highlight the stories of those heroes in our rich history who stood firm in their faith, even in the face of adversity. I plan to show how the faith of these men and women helped form the foundation of every major institution in this country. It was the faith of these great Americans that defeated slavery and gave women the right to vote. From establishing our legal system and educational institutions to developing social services and pursuing human rights, their unwavering belief in a higher purpose was instrumental in shaping the United States into the nation it is today.

You may be surprised to learn that many of these heroes didn't simply "fight the good fight." The men and women who built our nation weren't just warriors and scholars but also dreamers and poets. Those who have had the greatest impact on our nation didn't do so through grim determination alone but through laughter, creativity, and never-ending hope for a better future. They envisioned possibilities beyond their circumstances. In every era, it has been the dreamers and the poets, those who could see beyond the horizon of their present reality, who have propelled our country forward.

I don't plan to simply tell the stories of these American heroes. I aspire to break down exactly how they accomplished so much in one lifetime. I want to dive deep into their principles and habits. What made them successful where others fell short?

What choices did they make? How did they navigate failure and loss? How did they navigate success? By the end of this book, I hope to have discovered a road map to not just a better life but also a holier and healthier nation! In so doing, I believe what we learn will guide each and every reader to a more fulfilled and successful life. Each changed life will be yet another believer added to the fabric of our great nation. And every new hero will shift our national identity back to our founding principles.

This may sound like a lofty goal, but what is the point of believing for small things when you can believe for miracles? Like my grandmama and my mama, each of us can make choices that will shift the course of our lives, our families, our communities, our nation, and, ultimately, our world.

Part I

Vision

And afterward, I will pour out my Spirit on all people. Your sons and daughters will prophesy, your old men will dream dreams, your young men will see visions.

—JOEL 2:28

Chapter 1

A MORE PERFECT UNION

"He's one of these guys who, you know, he's like Clarence Thomas," Joy Behar said, "a Black Republican who believes in pulling yourself by your bootstraps, rather than, to me, understanding the systemic racism that African Americans face in this country and other minorities. He doesn't get it. Neither does Clarence. And that's why they're Republicans."

Behar said these words while hosting the morning talk show *The View*. Not for a moment did any of the other hosts—two of whom are African American—contradict her. In fact, the entire gaggle enthusiastically agreed.

This was nothing new. As a Black Republican, I have been labeled a "house nigger," a "sellout," a "disgrace," a "token," "Uncle Tim," a "race traitor," and the list goes on. The vileness and vitriol spewed mostly by white liberal elites are no longer astonishing. My focus makes me resilient. I am not surprised by these attacks and have learned to ignore them. I would say they were laughable if they weren't so dangerous.

Whenever I imagine a young boy or girl whose childhood

looks like mine, and I imagine them hearing those words, I can't hold back my disgust. Teaching our children of color that they are victims, that their present and future hold no hope, is dangerous and, dare I say, evil. To teach kids that their identity is found in the color of their skin is perverse, pure and simple. To tell an entire generation of young Americans of color that their life holds no hope or promise unless they are "the exception" is unbelievably vile. To tell them what to think because of their skin color is equally disgusting!

So I felt the need to respond to Joy Behar and the other hosts of *The View*. I offered to come on their show and speak with them. To my great surprise, they agreed. When I arrived at the studio, I noticed that Behar was conspicuously absent. Regardless, I have transcribed part of my interaction with another of the hosts, Sunny Hostin, below because I believe it directly ties in to one of the greatest lies facing our nation. Hostin is also Black. Over the first few minutes of the interview, she kept saying that she and I were "the exception to the rule." She clearly believes that America is still systemically racist and that Black kids don't have opportunities in America.

"One of the things I think about and one of the reasons why I'm on this show," I said, "is because of the comments that were made, frankly, on this show that the only way for a young African American kid to be successful in this country is to be the exception and not the rule. That is a dangerous, offensive, disgusting message to send to our young people today, that the only way to succeed is by being the exception. I will tell you that if my life is the exception, I can't imagine—"

"But it is," Hostin interrupted.

"But it's not, actually. The fact of the matter is, we've had an African American president, an African American vice president;

we've had two African Americans to be secretary of state. In my home city, the police chief is an African American who just won his race for mayor. The head of the highway patrol for South Carolina is an African American. In 1975, there was about 15 percent unemployment in the African American community; for the first time in the history of the country, it is under 5 percent nationally....

"So here's what I'm gonna suggest. I'm gonna suggest the fact of the matter is that progress in America is palpable. It can be measured in generations. I look back at the fact that my grandfather, born in 1921 in Sally, South Carolina, when he was on a sidewalk and a white person was coming, he had to step off and not make eye contact. That man believed then what some doubt now—in the goodness of America—because he believed that having faith in God, faith in himself, and faith in what the future could hold for his kids would unleash opportunities in ways that you cannot imagine. Every kid today can just change the station to see how much progress has been made in this country; ABC, NBC, CBS, ESPN, CNN, Fox News all have African American and Hispanic hosts. So what I'm suggesting is that yesterday's exception is today's rule."

"So America has met its promise?" Hostin interjected.

"The concept of America," I said, "is that we are going to become a more perfect union. But in fact, the challenges that we faced fifty years ago, and sixty years ago, should not be the same challenges that we face today."

I am going to stop here. If you would like to watch the whole interview, you can find it with a quick search, but Ms. Hostin's last question got my hackles up. When faced with absolute facts and sense, Ms. Hostin responded, "So America has met its promise?" This line most clearly defines the yawning gap between the Left and the Right in this country, between those who believe original sin defines America and those of us who believe the future will define us!

This kind of thinking stalls not just a life but a country. It epitomizes why so many people stagnate and eventually fail in life and why our nation remains so divided. By focusing solely on what's broken and ignoring the progress we've made, this mindset breeds a culture of victimhood rather than empowerment.

So *has* America met its promise? Let me translate this for you. In the next chapter, I plan to share the story of William Lloyd Garrison, who was almost lynched for his beliefs in 1835. From that day to today, the list of victories is impressive. Consider the Emancipation Proclamation (1863); the 13th, 14th, and 15th Amendments (1865–1870); *Brown v. Board of Education* (1954); the Civil Rights Act (1964); the Voting Rights Act (1965); and the Fair Housing Act (1968). The progress we have made on the issue of race is truly astounding.

Each of the milestones mentioned above addressed significant injustices. Yet Ms. Hostin would have you believe that things are still nearly as bad as they were in 1835. When faced with progress, all she can see is what isn't working. When she and the other hosts of *The View* look at our country, they see only victims and brokenness. Under the guise of "empathy," they relegate an entire generation to victimhood, ignoring the progress we have made as a nation. My life is not an exception. I am the product of a praying, hardworking mother and the opportunities afforded by this great nation.

The idea behind Ms. Hostin's comment carries a kernel of truth—which is why the lie spreads so quickly. No, we have not arrived in the perfect country yet. If you look for it, you will find injustice that needs to be weeded out. Yes, as the old saying goes, "We aren't where we should be, but thank God almighty we aren't where we used to be!" There will always be more work to do. That doesn't negate the fact that no country on earth is freer or more filled with opportunities than the United States of America.

The preamble to the Constitution reads, "We the People of the United States, in Order to form a more perfect Union, establish Justice, insure domestic Tranquility, provide for the common defense, promote the general Welfare, and secure the Blessings of Liberty to ourselves and our Posterity, do ordain and establish this Constitution for the United States of America."

"To form a more perfect union"—this is America meeting her promise! To answer Ms. Hostin's question clearly, yes, America has met her promise. And yes, she will continue to do so. We must not paint an entire generation as victims simply because we have further to go.

One hundred years ago, very little progress had been made in addressing the original sin of our nation—the sin of slavery. Yet even in those darkest times, countless champions emerged, willing to sacrifice everything to bring about true and lasting justice. These courageous individuals were the lights shining in the darkness, providing reason for hope. I could recount thousands of stories of the men and women who fought tirelessly to end slavery. However, one story has always stood out to me: the story of a man who would not compromise, no matter the cost. This is the story of William Lloyd Garrison.

Lessons Learned

ACKNOWLEDGING PROGRESS IS ESSENTIAL TO MOVING FORWARD. The contrast between those who focus on what is broken and those who acknowledge progress is clear. While some view America as stagnant in its journey toward equality, the reality is that the country has made significant strides over the decades, with major milestones in civil rights and justice. Recognizing this progress allows us to continue improving rather than being trapped in a mindset of victimhood.

FOCUSING ON PROGRESS DOES NOT DENY PROBLEMS. It is hope for the future that gives us the power to fight against injustice today! Hope fuels our resilience, reminding us that our efforts, no matter how small, contribute to building a better tomorrow. It inspires us to persevere in the face of obstacles, knowing that the change we seek begins with the actions we take right now.

HISTORICAL ACHIEVEMENTS ARE A TESTAMENT TO AMERICA'S GREATNESS. There have been countless milestones in American history. The Emancipation Proclamation and the Civil Rights Act, to name just two, illustrate that America has been steadily working toward fulfilling its promise of justice and equality. While challenges remain, these achievements show that progress is ongoing, and each generation must continue to build on these foundations to create a more perfect union.

The first step toward restoring the faith of our nation is recovering a vision for its future. We can't do that if we're determined to deny that change is possible, or to not take joy in the achievements that exist. Vision requires us to believe that we have agency and responsibility. Victimhood kills vision. With that in mind, let's look back at the story of someone who truly found a vision when change seemed impossible.

Chapter 2

WILLIAM LLOYD GARRISON

If the Truth Is on Your Side, Stand Firm

October 21, 1835

William Lloyd Garrison placed a fist on the small of his back, digging in to try to work out the knot that had formed there. He'd spent the early part of the week writing the articles. That was the easy part of his job. When your mission consumes you, words come easy. The painstaking task of typesetting, the days spent arranging every last letter, complete with the wooden spacers, was cumbersome. As he stepped back to assess his handiwork, his hand went unbidden to the lump on his forehead. With each passing week, the danger grew.

William had published the first printing of his newspaper, *The Liberator*, four years earlier; from the very first days, it hadn't been easy, yet the past few months had been particularly hard. In truth, William saw the growing danger as proof that he was making a difference, that success was nearer than ever. If so many people saw him as a threat, that had to mean he was changing hearts and minds. Surely, the country was closer to redemption than it had ever been. *At least I'm not being ignored*; the thought brought a small smile to his lips.

Ever since his first printing, William had become used to angry glares, but in the past months, he'd been spat on or yelled at more times than he could count. As his readership grew, so too did the threats of violence against him. This week's paper lambasted the Fugitive Slave Law, which imposed severe penalties on those who helped runaway slaves and mandated that officials and citizens of free states must cooperate in the capture and return of fugitive slaves to their "owners." William's blood boiled at the sheer madness of it.

William lived in the free state of Massachusetts, where slavery was outlawed. Even so, most of his fellow residents did not share his abolitionist views. William believed that slavery was a sin against God and humanity. Yet he lived in a country where his president, Andrew Jackson, was a plantation owner from Tennessee.

While it was true that Massachusetts had officially outlawed slavery more than fifty years earlier, countless people still preached its virtues. In one of this week's articles, William quoted scripture, as he often did. William believed in Jesus of Nazareth. He believed that the word of God was a beacon of unyielding light amid the encroaching shadow. In a world often mired in ambiguity and uncertainty, William saw the Bible as a compass, directing hearts and minds toward a higher calling and a deeper understanding of the divine.

He needed to give the article one final proofread before he began the printing process. William donned his spectacles, leaned in close, and read aloud.

> *In my heart and in my writings, I have consistently implored my fellow citizens and Christians to recognize the grave sin that is slavery and to act swiftly to abolish it. It is not merely a matter of politics or economy but a profound moral and spiritual crisis that afflicts our nation and our souls.*

> Is not this the fast that I choose: to loose the bonds of wickedness, to undo the straps of the yoke, to let the oppressed go free, and to break every yoke?
> —Isaiah 58:6, ESV

William was powered by a steely sense of the righteousness of his cause. He tolerated no compromise and promoted a fiery vision of nonviolent resistance. His paper shredded the flimsy defenses of slavery advocates.

One writer scorned those who resorted to invoking the Bible "to support 'a system of oppression, fornication, adultery and murder.'" He declared this a "Fine use of" the Bible. "Are these gentlemen in the habit of going to it for any other purpose? We should think not, otherwise that would be better acquainted with it than to name it in such a connexion."[1]

William knew that the truth was on his side. But his faith was about to receive its greatest test. It's easy to have principles on paper, but what proves their reality is if they survive when it takes a cost.

On the day of October 21, William had gone to the Boston Female Anti-Slavery Society to give a speech. Trouble was brewing. While Boston was a long way from the plantation society of the Deep South, much of its economy still depended on the status quo's remaining in place. The faith of a man like William was a direct challenge to this reality.

As he stepped through the Anti-Slavery Society's doors, William must have noticed that more people were in the streets than normal. There was an air of frenzied excitement on the faces of the men loitering outside. They weren't poor men or criminals, but rather gentlemen. Lawyers, doctors, clerks. Acting on a false tip that a controversial British abolitionist, George Thompson, was slated to speak, a mob of these privileged men were gathered outside. The Boston mayor, feeling rather harassed by his own supporters, told them that Thompson was not even in the city, but the crowd didn't listen. They were out for blood, and if they couldn't have Thompson, they'd find somebody else.

That's when they saw William. Bespectacled and balding, William was not an imposing man, but he wasn't easily intimidated. Plus, he had a mischievous sense of humor. Seeing the men lingering on the doorstep, he decided to poke the bear.

He walked over to a few of them. "Gentlemen, perhaps you are not aware that this is a meeting of the Boston *Female* Anti-Slavery Society, called and intended exclusively for *ladies*, and those only who have been invited to address them."

Smiling, he went on, "If, gentlemen, any of you are ladies in disguise, why, only apprise me of the fact, give me your names, and I will introduce you to the rest of your sex, and you can take seats among them accordingly."[2]

Somewhat shamed, the men retreated for a while, but William could see that things were only going to get worse. The voices outside grew more and more heated. The word had passed from the men he'd just spoken with to a more radical bunch. "Garrison! Garrison! We must have Garrison! Out with him! Lynch him!" Men grabbed the wooden "Anti-Slavery Society" sign from over the doorway and threw it to the ground, where it was instantly stomped into splinters by the mob. The mayor's entreaties seemed frail against the crowd's fury.

Crash! The sound of breaking glass startled William from his thoughts. He was terrified! Maybe escape was possible. With the voices echoing around the corner of the building, William made for a back window, diving through onto a shed and from there to the ground. Unprepared for the uneven dirt, he nearly sprawled to the ground, but he regained his balance.

The next moments were pure chaos. He dashed into a carpenter's shop through the back entrance, heading for the street, but immediately shouts went up from rioters on the other side. "Lynch him! Lynch him!"

He fled, darting into an alleyway, his breath coming now in ragged gasps. How could this be happening in Boston, the birthplace of liberty? Despite his panic, William felt a keen sense of intellectual outrage.

Ducking into a doorway, he staggered up the stairs, then cast about desperately for a hiding place. No use—the sound of pounding footsteps on the stairs underlined the truth: There was no way out. Heart pounding, William turned to face the clutch of rioters.

The men seized him, yelling with maniacal glee that they had found the dirty slave-loving abolitionist. Roughly, he was dragged toward the window, where the high drop to the cobblestones awaited. "Wait!" One of the men pointed out that this was too quick and easy a fate. They had a better idea.

One of the men shoved William back and pulled something

out of his bag. With dawning horror, William realized that one man was coiling a rope about his body, preparing to drag him through the streets like a spectacle from some barbaric medieval execution.

He had to think fast. Sensing the impulsive confusion of his captors, William pointed to a ladder that someone had raised to the window. "Allow me to climb down," he said. "You can have me."

Something in his voice seemed to break their concentration—they obediently bundled him out the window. Now it was time for a tricky maneuver. As he climbed down the ladder, William moved slowly, giving himself time to disentangle and lose the rope—stepping onto the ground, he left the mob only the option of grabbing him, a move that probably saved his life.

But now there was nothing between him and the mob. Two burly rioters clamped their hands onto William's shoulders and dragged him along. His hat was knocked from his head and quickly chopped to bits. Enraged rioters swung at William's bare head and clutched at his clothes. He felt the cloth ripping away from his body and was horrified to realize that the men had stripped him mostly nude.

Slowly, awareness arose in William Lloyd Garrison. This was actually a lynching. He was being dragged to the town square, where he would be hanged for all to see. Strangely, in what should have been a terrifying moment, William was not afraid. He closed his eyes and tried to breathe steadily.

Scattered on the ground were the torn and tattered pages of prayer books that the mob, assuming them to be abolitionist tracts, had destroyed. The feet of the "respectable" men trampled psalms and prayers into the mud. In a way, William thought amid his shock, they were right: Those tracts were the very source of abolitionism, of man's infinite value in the eyes of God.

The gathered mob continued their shouts of rage as they reached the square. Grimly, William overheard the confused mob debating whether to tar and feather him or drown him in the pond. Everywhere William looked, there was only hatred.[3]

Calls of "Lynch the slave lover!" and "String him up!" came from everywhere. It was chaos.

"Hey!" The shout broke through the cacophony as the mayor returned, this time with a posse of men whom he'd rallied to William's aid. The burly men elbowed through the crowd of rioters and dragged William to safety, bundling him into a waiting carriage, which began to gallop away.

Still, the crowd attempted to seize him. William would later write,

> *As the ocean, lashed into fury by the spirit of the storm, seeks to whelm the adventurous bark beneath its mountain waves — so did the mob, enraged by a series of disappointments, rush like a whirlwind upon the frail vehicle in which I sat, and endeavor to drag me out of it. Escape seemed a physical impossibility. They clung to the wheels — dashed open the doors — seized hold of the horses — and tried to upset the carriage.*[4]

A policeman leapt into the carriage and battered back the crowd, while the driver whipped at horses and rioters alike to keep the waves at bay. Back and forth they wound through the streets of Boston, escaping by a hair's breadth several dead ends and traps. At last the jail was in sight. The carriage pulled to a screeching halt and William dashed out, narrowly avoiding the pursuers, who'd anticipated their destination, and into the jail.

Finally, William was safe. He was put under arrest as a disturber of the peace. As the adrenaline wore off, he found himself surprisingly calm. Cheerfully, he spent the evening rejoicing in his deliverance and proudly defiant of the mob's power. He scratched this on the wall of this cell:

Wm. Lloyd Garrison was put into this cell on Wednesday afternoon, Oct. 21, 1835, to save him from the violence of 'a respectable and influential' mob, who sought to destroy him for preaching the abominable and dangerous doctrine, that 'all men are created equal,' and that all oppression is odious in the sight of God.

Despite the failures of the society around him, William's faith in God buoyed him through danger and threat. He knew that in the end, the truth would always win. With it on his side, he could do nothing else but stand firm. Of this trial, paraphrasing Scripture (Romans 5:3), he wrote, "In the midst of tribulation, therefore, we rejoice, and count it all honor to suffer in the cause of our dear Redeemer."[5]

* * *

William Lloyd Garrison spent a night in jail, not as a criminal but as a man under the protective custody of the mayor, believed to be the only safe haven amid threats of lynching. Yet this harrowing experience only fueled his determination. An unyielding abolitionist, Garrison was guided by a profound conviction that his cause was not just right but righteous. Driven by the Holy Spirit, he stood firm, uncompromising in the face of danger.

"I am in earnest—I will not equivocate—I will not excuse—I will not retreat a single inch—AND I WILL BE HEARD." These words adorned the front page of the very first printing of Garrison's newspaper, *The Liberator*. I love everything about this. When you possess truth and hold the answers to life's most profound questions, you are compelled to speak. William Lloyd Garrison was compelled to speak! Truth burned inside his soul, and silence was not an option. To hold the light and not cast it into the shadows would be the definition of injustice.

Today, the word "truth" has become a casualty of cultural relativism. Phrases like "Live your truth" or "This is my truth" have diluted its meaning, rendering it almost irrelevant. But truth is not subjective. While there are many shades of gray on various issues, there remains only one objective truth. Moral relativism has no place in matters of fundamental truth.

We must stand firm in our convictions and uphold these truths, not just for ourselves but for the generations to come. It's essential to teach our children that while perspectives and opinions can vary, truth is steadfast. This is not just about winning a cultural war; it's about preserving the integrity of our nation and ensuring that we continue to uphold the principles that have guided us since our founding.

William Lloyd Garrison never compromised on the truth, even when faced with overwhelming opposition. His unwavering stance against slavery and his relentless pursuit of justice remind us that standing firm in our convictions can lead to monumental change. Just as Garrison did not give in to the pressures of his time, we, too, must hold steadfast to the truths that define us, regardless of the cultural tides that seek to wash them away.

As I have crisscrossed our great nation over the past many months, I have heard the lies corroding our country's very foundation. Evil is more brazen than I have ever seen it. We need William Lloyd Garrisons. We require William Lloyd Garrisons. America needs men and women of true character who will not compromise, no matter the consequences. As a people, we have been given the key. As a country, we have a guide to life's most profound questions. When I pick up my Bible, I am holding a road map for life. Our nation was founded on the Gospel of Jesus. Our Founding Fathers had blind spots, and they were not without sin. However, the core of our founding was strong because it was based on the teachings of Jesus Christ.

I love the story of William Lloyd Garrison because he never once threw a punch or advocated violence. He was unyielding and fought with truth. He refused to back down even when it meant his very life. William Lloyd Garrison understood that light will defeat darkness every time.

Lessons Learned

STANDING FIRM IN OUR CONVICTIONS IS ESSENTIAL FOR CREATING LASTING CHANGE. William Lloyd Garrison's unwavering commitment to abolition, even in the face of violence and near death, exemplifies the power of holding fast to our beliefs. His refusal to retreat, despite the dangers, serves as a reminder that monumental change often requires us to stand resolute in our convictions, no matter the opposition. William really was seen as a "disturber of the peace" by his enemies. That's the sort of mistaken diagnosis you make when your idea of peace is actually oppression of and cruelty toward people made in the image of God, your fellow image-bearers. Despite being attacked and nearly lynched, William continued his work, knowing that his cause was just. His courage under pressure not only advanced the abolitionist movement but also served as an inspiration for others to speak out against injustice.

TRUTH IS NOT SUBJECTIVE. William believed deeply in the objective truth that slavery was a moral wrong. In today's world, phrases like "my truth" have become common, but truth is not flexible or relative! William's dedication to fighting for universal truth reminds us that there are some principles—like justice and freedom—that should not be compromised.

FAITH IS A GUIDING FORCE WHEN STANDING FOR JUSTICE. William's belief in God and the teachings of Jesus Christ were the source of his resolve to fight against slavery. His faith gave him the strength to endure hardship and remain steadfast in his mission.

Chapter 3

TRAINING A GODLY IMAGINATION

Standing up for the truth is essential to the progress of a country. But how do we know what truth is? Many today would tell you that it's not possible to know. I started to understand truth in an unusual way, at a game many years ago.

"Seven! Hut! Hut! Hut!" Thomas's words held the power of creation. His simple command set into motion the play that would change my life forever.

Snap!

I explode from my stance, feinting right, then cutting left into open space. The scoreboard reads 16–10 with eight seconds left on the clock in the fourth quarter. We are down; this is our final play, our Hail Mary.

From fifteen yards away, Thomas—my quarterback—meets my eyes as his arm cocks back, releasing a bullet pass that rockets toward me. With perfect precision, I extend my hands, feeling the leather slide in through my fingers as I pull the football close to my chest.

I run at an all-out sprint, crashing through the defense like a wrecking ball. Every step is perfection. I can feel it in my bones. This play will be talked about for the next twenty years or longer. Even as I run, I catch a glimpse of Sophia, the girl I secretly like. A short distance behind her, I can see my mother and my aunt cheering wildly. Every one of the thousands of fans is on their feet, screaming at the tops of their lungs.

I play wide receiver, and my name is known three states over. The other teams call me Tim the Destroyer. I am the most feared young man on the team. *Keep your head in the game, Scott,* I berate myself. *Don't get cocky!*

Suddenly, I pivot, darting toward the sideline. One defender lunges, but I shrug him off, adrenaline fueling my run. I cut back to the middle as a second defender attempts to wrap me up, but I spin, his grasp slipping off.

The end zone is in sight. Every last man, woman, and child in the stands is on their feet, cheering and chanting my name. Suddenly, everything shifts, the world moving as if in slow motion. Even amid my breathless run, I can't help but smile. When the world slows down like this, there is no stopping me. It's like I can see the future and react with split-second timing.

Two defenders stand between me and glory. As I reach the first, I lower my shoulder, smashing through him like a freight train, never slowing. The second defender dives at my feet as I near the end zone. Thinking fast, I plant one foot and launch myself into the air, performing a somersault over the diving player. As I flip, I see the goal line pass beneath me. I land just over it, the ball firmly secured.

Touchdown!

The crowd roars, and with that, the feeling of euphoria rises, a moment of football magic etched in the collective memory of everyone there. My teammates surround me, lifting me to their shoulders. I'll never forget the look of absolute pride in Coach's eyes. It was clear that I was the son he'd always wanted.

When my team finally brings me down from their shoulders, I am barely able to catch my balance before a hand grabs my shoulder and spins me around. It's Sophia! She is standing directly in front of me. My breath catches. At best, I am awkward with girls. Before I can get a word out, Sophia steps forward and kisses me on the cheek.

I blink, and everything fades away. I am in the bed I share with my mother and my brother in the cramped room of my grandparents' rental. The entire scene had played out in my eight-year-old mind as I lay there, letting my imagination run wild. Even though I knew it wasn't real, I couldn't help but grin. "It's going to happen," I whisper to the ceiling. "I will make it real!"

"What are you going on about, Timmy?" Ben whispers. "You know if you wake Mama, she'll tan your hide."

I turn to my ten-year-old brother, who has always been my hero. "I'm going to be the best football player this world has ever seen," I whisper to Ben.

Ben stares at me for a long moment. "You just started playing last year. Maybe start thinking about being the best player on your team first," he whispers. Finally, after a long moment, he says, "But I don't doubt it, Timmy. You will be great. Now go to sleep!"

***

My most vivid memories are not of learning to ride a bike, skinning my knees, or blowing out birthday candles. Instead, what sticks out most are the hours I spent staring at the ceiling. My favorite part of my day often happened after I crawled into bed. The countless hours I spent inside my head, inside my wild imagination, fueled me to face the next day.

When I say I grew up poor, most who read that line will have no frame of reference for what I actually mean. After all, there are many levels of poverty. While my mother, brother, and I may not have been on the bottom rung of the socioeconomic ladder, at best, we were only a rung or two up. I am not lamenting my childhood. I have the most unbelievable memories from when I was young. More important than anything, my brother, Ben, and I were loved. My mama sacrificed her entire world so that we could have a better life.

Mama never once thought of us as "poor." She never lamented our lack. Though we went without more often than not, she never considered herself or her boys victims. When faced with impossible adversity, Mama merely dreamed bigger and worked harder. My mama, Frances, worked harder than anyone I have ever known, except for maybe her own mother!

I mention the poverty of my childhood because it played a role in forming my imagination. When you don't have anything, your imagination becomes everything. Every night when I lay in bed, staring at the ceiling, my life became something extraordinary, something magical. The girl I secretly liked didn't care about my spectacularly skewed front teeth, and she still wanted to kiss me. As I stared at the ceiling, I saw myself sprinting down the football field, with everyone cheering and shouting my name.

The ceiling was my portal to a world so far out of reach that it was laughable. I often tell people that I am the embodiment of the American Dream. In any other country in the world, I would still be standing at the bottom of the socioeconomic ladder. Yet here in the United States, I grew up surrounded by something magical. And it is this very magic that makes our country the greatest nation on earth. The magic that changed my life can be defined in one word: "opportunity."

I don't care what your circumstances might be or what rung of the ladder you find yourself on; if you have the eyes to see it, the imagination to breathe life into it, and the work ethic to not give up, there is opportunity all around you!

Christians are sometimes wary of imagination, thinking it's just a word for making things up. C. S. Lewis knew better. He pointed out that while our imagination certainly can lead us into foolish escapism, it's also what he called the "organ of meaning." It takes the hard facts of what we know and do and the dreams of our heart and soul and melds them in order to reveal what's possible. How else can we turn the unreal into the real? When Jesus told parables, it was because He knew that human beings could learn things through our imagination that we couldn't learn any other way. To create a new life, we first have to imagine it. To bring about the kingdom of God, Jesus knew He first had to persuade his disciples to imagine it.

I don't downplay or belittle the power of hard work. But true success is not merely the product of tireless effort. While hard work is undoubtedly important, the power of imagination breathes life into our endeavors and brings about something magical—purpose.

I eventually became the best football player on my team. I experienced large crowds chanting my name as I helped carry the team to many victories. In my junior year, scouts watched me play, and I was beginning to receive attention that would lead to scholarship offers. If not for a spectacularly brutal car crash that almost ended my life and absolutely ended any hope of continuing with football, I would have been on track to accomplish my dreams.

My wild imaginings are no longer as fantastical or juvenile as they were when I was eight, but I still lie in bed and dream with God. The older I got, the more I realized that this is exactly what happens when I stare at the ceiling. God made me. It was God who gave me this fantastic imagination. Together, each and every night, God and I imagine what the future holds.

I believe that the power of imagination is one of the most extraordinary gifts God has given humanity. Your imagination has the potential to transform your life in profound ways. Every innovation and invention began as a collaboration between divine inspiration and human creativity. Every significant leap forward in human history was born from someone's imagination.

You may wonder why I am writing about the power of the imagination. In a previous chapter, I made it clear that we are in a battle for our nation's soul. Great darkness presses against the light, and before we can experience redemption, there must be a reckoning! What does imagination have to do with anything?

Imagination and prayer are intertwined. They go hand in hand, like wet and water. Without imagination, prayer can quickly become an empty ritual. And without an active and intimate prayer life, there is no meaningful relationship with our Creator. Our faith is birthed out of spending time with God, out of prayer. So hear me when I say that a God-given, wild imagination is incredibly important! Prayer speaks light into darkness, life into death, and hope into despair. Prayer connects us to the heartbeat of God. Prayer allows us to see others as God sees them.

When we look around, we see plenty of evidence of imagination gone wrong. So many young people seem to be totally out of touch with their created selves and will chase every stray thought to its conclusion, regardless of the cost. That's why the Bible talks about subjecting our minds and our hearts to the Word. In Romans 12:2, Paul advises, "Do not conform to the pattern of this world, but be transformed by the renewing of your mind. Then you will be able to test and approve what God's will is—his good, pleasing and perfect will."

Imagination isn't the problem. God gave us the ability to imagine, and He sends us our every dream. As with all our faculties, however, we must work to align these gifts with the will of God and not our own sinful desires.

When we align our hearts with the heart of God, our dreams are His dreams. Faith transforms our deepest hopes into something sacred, shaping the prayers we don't even have to speak aloud. When we dream with God and let our imagination run wild with His thoughts, we begin to see a way forward where none seemed possible.

I have met countless men, women, and children who struggle to pray. *Am I talking too much? Am I asking for too much? Am I listening enough? When I listen, my mind often wanders, and quite honestly, I don't know if I have ever heard God in the first place!*

I've heard preachers I respect speak on the power of prayer more times than I can count, but sometimes their eagerness to emphasize its importance makes it sound impossibly daunting. *Prayer is everything! It is our connection with the Creator! It is an intimate connection with God! And it is a mystery we can never understand!*

But what if it isn't? What if prayer is as easy as breathing? What if Jesus is our friend and prayer is an intimate conversation with our friend? What if God gave us our dreams, our wild and vivid imaginations? What if this is one of the key ways in which He speaks to us? What if our dreams are the prayers we dream with God? When I stare at the ceiling and align my heart with the Holy Spirit, His dreams become my dreams.

Think about it. How else are we meant to connect with the Creator of the universe? Through our needs? Through desperation? Through listening with all we have and not really knowing if we've heard anything? Hear me. I am not making light of traditional prayer. I am on my knees every morning. I pray for my family and for this nation daily. I believe that my prayers don't have a shelf life. I believe that my prayers make a difference in the world! But for so many, prayer feels like a task or something to check off on the day's to-do list. But what if prayer is actually the most exciting part of our lives? What if prayer taps into the most beautiful parts of existence? What if prayer is dreaming with God? What if prayer is our wildest imaginings connecting to God's dreams for us?

Each and every one of us has dreams that God has woven into our hearts. Yet so many of us have pushed down these dreams for hundreds of reasons. But what happens when we dream—with God? What happens when we dream together as a nation?

The answer is simple: We have almost 250 years of dreaming together. When we dreamed together as a nation, slavery was ended. When the collective imagination and dreams of Americans converged, we achieved monumental feats such as securing women the right to vote. A dream that once seemed absurd eventually led to our putting the first man on the moon.

The prayers, dreams, and imagination of our Founding Fathers established the greatest nation on earth. Their vision and faith laid the groundwork for a country built on liberty, justice, and equality. These same prayers, dreams, and imaginings continue to shape our nation through the efforts of countless men and women who forged our healthcare system, educational institutions, infrastructure, and military.

Lessons Learned

IMAGINATION FUELS OUR DREAMS. It gives us the ability to envision a future beyond our current circumstances. When I was little, my imagination allowed me to escape the harsh realities of poverty and picture myself surrounded by success. Regardless of where we start in life, our ability to imagine something better can be the first step toward achieving it. Imagination is a tool that opens up possibilities and helps us craft a vision for the future that can guide our actions.

FAITH IS CLOSELY LINKED TO OPPORTUNITY. I have always believed that my dreams could become reality, reflecting the belief that in America, opportunity is available to those who are willing to imagine it and work for it. I cannot stress the importance of seeing beyond immediate limitations and recognizing the potential for growth and success through perseverance and vision. Imagination allows us to identify the hidden opportunities around us, even in challenging circumstances.

FAITH AND PRAYER ARE INTERCONNECTED. Prayer is more than a formal conversation with God; it is an invitation to dream with Him. If we can see prayer through this lens, it transforms our prayer times into a dynamic process of aligning our imaginations with God's will, where our deepest dreams and hopes are intertwined with divine inspiration. It teaches us that faith and imagination together can lead to profound change, making prayer an avenue to explore and pursue our greatest aspirations.

Chapter 4

FRED FOX

Do Your Best Even When No One Knows

It's easy to do your job when you have an adoring audience. But how do we go about fulfilling God's plan for us when it doesn't look like how we dreamed it would? The laughter of the crowd fills our hearts—we all have a space within us that wants to be praised.

Fred Fox certainly felt that. He graduated from Princeton in 1939. While at the prestigious university, Fred was a devout Christian and a member of the Princeton Triangle Club, the oldest collegiate musical comedy troupe in the nation. He also fancied himself a comedian, which is how he first caught the eye of Hannah Putnam. Hannah and Fred met after one of his performances, and it was love at first laugh. It wasn't long before they were engaged.

Fred dreamed of performing in front of large audiences and maybe even appearing in a big-screen movie someday. The year

1939 is still referred to as the golden age of film. *Gone With the Wind* and *The Wizard of Oz* were released in Technicolor, and movies were forever changed. Yet Fred and Hannah's dreams were shattered on December 7, 1941, when the first bombs were dropped on Pearl Harbor, and the United States of America officially entered World War II.

Fred and Hannah decided to get married after the war. Before he shipped out, Fred and Hannah prayed together. After a kiss and a loving embrace, Fred was shipped overseas, and like many women who were left behind, Hannah contributed by volunteering to head up blood drives and recruit nurses.

Fred, ever the entertainer, had always had a knack for practical jokes. While at Princeton, he was likely involved in a scheme with other students to invent a fictional classmate with the implausible name "Ephraim di Kahble," and have him place a series of elaborate advertisements in the school paper promising things like paying an extravagant amount for a seat at a home game. The jig was up, however, when they tried to get the imaginary character elected treasurer of the freshman class and placed an ad in the *New York Times*.[6] Fred's sense of humor about the incident remained intact, however: Years later, he wrote a piece for the school paper remembering fondly, as an alumni, all the days he spent with his old classmate, "the Hon. Ephraim di Kahble, OTB, of Tezcatlipoca, Mexico."[7]

So perhaps, with this personality, it's not surprising that in January 1944, Captain Fred Fox was recruited into a special top secret unit that had just been created. Only eleven hundred men were recruited, and when they were first brought together, Fred wondered if this was some kind of joke.

"Officially," Colonel Harry L. Reeder, the commanding officer, told the men, "we are known as the 23rd Headquarters Special Troops. Unofficially, we are the Ghost Army."

Fred and many of the other men laughed until they realized that Colonel Reeder wasn't joking. Over the next weeks, the men trained not as soldiers but as artists. Their purpose was not to be an actual army but to *appear* to be an actual army in order to deceive the enemy about the real army's location. Over the ensuing months, the Ghost Army participated in over twenty operations across Europe. Their efforts were crucial in several key operations, including the Normandy landings, the Battle of the Bulge, and the crossing of the Rhine River, ultimately saving countless lives and contributing significantly to the Allied victory in World War II.

What did the Ghost Army do? They were tasked with performing magic acts, creating the biggest illusions the world had ever seen. The men were provided with hundreds of inflatable tanks, trucks, jeeps, artillery, and even aircraft. These detailed decoys were designed to be realistic enough to deceive aerial reconnaissance and ground observers. The unit also created fake buildings, such as command posts and supply depots, to add to the illusion of a significant military presence.

Along with the visual deception, they also utilized audio trickery, such as playing recorded sounds of troop movements, construction, and other military activities through powerful speakers.

At first, Fred was deeply unimpressed with his men. They didn't seem to understand the spirit of the thing. Their shoddy efforts at creating an illusion struck him as "bad theater."

"The attitude of the 23rd HQs towards their mission is lopsided," he wrote in a memo to command. "There is too much

MILITARY ... and not enough SHOWMANSHIP," he observed. "Like it or not, the 23rd HQ must consider itself a traveling road show."[8]

Surprisingly, Fred's tart note was embraced by his superiors. They allowed him to enhance the Ghost Army's efforts with special effects of his own. He trained his men as actors, instructing them to dress as the unit they were impersonating and to be ready to answer questions about it if asked by civilians.

"Behind every operation was a touch of Fred Fox," one of his men remembered. "He'd get us in a huddle and say, 'This is what's going to happen, and this is what we want you to say, and just be natural.' For example, guys went to the bakery, got some rolls, and said, 'We've got to get an extra supply because we're moving out tonight,' that kind of thing."

These comprehensive deception strategies allowed the Ghost Army to simulate the presence of large forces, effectively misleading the German military.

Fred insisted that his men even impersonate generals, since there couldn't possibly be a better way of persuading the Germans that the Ghost Army was important than to give the impression that the top brass were present. "Is not the whole idea of 'impersonation' contrary to [Army regulations]?" he wrote. This didn't bother him. "Remember we are in the theater business. Impersonation is our racket. If we can't do a complete job we might as well give up. You can't portray a woman if bosoms are forbidden."[9]

It was March 1945, and the final months of World War II were proving to be some of the most crucial. The Allied forces were preparing for one of their most significant operations: crossing the Rhine River into Germany. The Ghost Army was once again called upon to play a critical role in this effort.

The operation, code-named "Operation Viersen," aimed to create the illusion of a massive Allied force preparing to cross the Rhine at a location ten miles from the actual crossing point. This deception was intended to divert German attention and resources, allowing the real 9th Army to make their move with minimal resistance.

Fred Fox had two hundred men under his command. At this point in the war, the Ghost Army worked like a well-oiled machine. Fred went over the plan with his men in meticulous detail.

"Men," he said, "this will be our biggest mission yet. We need to set up more than six hundred inflatable tanks, artillery pieces, and trucks along a ten-mile stretch of the Rhine."

Several of his men gasped audibly.

Fred ignored them. "These decoys must be convincing from ground and air. We also need to build at least twenty fake buildings and command posts to create the illusion of a massive Allied force prepping to cross the river." Fred felt the weight of the mission. He waited a moment, meeting the eyes of many of his men. "Meanwhile, the real crossing is ten miles away, where the 9th Army will cross the Rhine. If we do our jobs well, we'll keep the Germans' attention on us, and the 9th will meet minimal resistance, which means what?"

"Fewer casualties," the men said together.

"Significantly fewer casualties," Fred repeated. "And once the 9th has crossed, there will no longer be a barrier between the Allies and Nazi Germany. If our brothers-in-arms can cross this river, the Allied forces can finally push west toward Berlin."

Fred clapped his hands together. "Now," he said with a small smile, "let us pray."

Most of the men had some level of faith and knelt to pray with their captain. The men who were less religious or simply didn't believe in God at all still respected their brothers enough to listen respectfully. The aphorism "There are no atheists in foxholes" is famous for a reason.[10]

The preparation for this elaborate deception took several weeks, during which all eleven hundred men of the Ghost Army meticulously planned and set up their inflatables, sound equipment, and fake radio transmissions. This extensive effort included creating realistic sounds of troop movements and bridge construction, which played day and night to enhance the illusion.

Fred worked closely with the unit's sound technicians to set up massive loudspeakers hidden among the trees and buildings. These speakers played recorded sounds of rumbling tanks, marching soldiers, and the clatter of equipment, creating an auditory illusion of an impending attack.

The unit also employed fake radio transmissions, complete with coded messages and chatter, to simulate the communications of a large army. Fred was tasked with ensuring that these transmissions were convincing and coordinated with the visual and auditory deceptions.

As night fell on March 23, 1945, the Ghost Army's preparations were complete. Fred Fox and his fellow soldiers waited in silence. If the Germans discovered the ruse too soon, the entire operation would be compromised, and their brothers, who were crossing the river ten miles to the south, would be sitting ducks.

The Germans had been closely monitoring Allied movements and were on high alert. Any mistake could be disastrous. Fred moved through the shadows, checking and rechecking the inflatables and sound equipment to ensure that everything was in place.

At dawn, the Germans launched a reconnaissance flight over

the area. The Ghost Army's inflatables and sound effects were in full operation. From the air, the Germans saw what appeared to be a massive buildup of Allied forces. Inflatable tanks and artillery pieces were strategically placed to mimic a real division preparing for an assault. The sounds of engines and marching soldiers added to the illusion, creating a convincing picture of a large army on the move.

Fred watched as the German plane flew overhead. His heart pounded with a mix of fear and excitement. "God," Fred whispered, "this is the biggest performance of my life." He smiled at the idea. "Please let the audience believe it!"

If the deception worked, it would give the 9th Army the opportunity they needed to cross the river with minimal resistance. If it failed, the consequences would be dire.

As the reconnaissance plane passed, Fred received a signal from his commanding officer, Captain Ralph Ingersoll, confirming that the Germans had taken the bait. The Ghost Army's deception was working. The German forces began repositioning troops and resources to the other side of the Rhine to counter the perceived threat!

With the Germans diverted, the 9th Army began its assault on the Rhine at Remagen. Thanks to the Ghost Army's successful deception, they encountered far less resistance than expected. The crossing was a critical step in the Allied advance into Germany, paving the way for the final push toward Berlin.

Fred Fox and his men continued their deception for several more days, maintaining the illusion of a large force preparing for an attack. They moved their inflatables and sound equipment to new positions, keeping the Germans off-balance and uncertain about the Allies' true intentions.

Eight days after the end of World War II, Captain Fred

Fox married the love of his life, Hannah Putnam. Though he never appeared on the big screen, he did become a minister, and years later, he worked as a special assistant to President Dwight Eisenhower.

But one suspects the performance that was most important to him was the invisible one. The Ghost Army's actions were so secret that most members of the regular army didn't know the unit existed, and the men were not recognized for their heroism after the war. However, in an attempt to capture the meaning of their efforts, Fred wrote this:

> *The 23rd Headquarters Special Troops has probably been associated with more Armies and been to more places than any other unit aboard ship. Some of its members landed on D-day with the First Army.... The itinerary of the 23rd sounds like a roll call of famous place names.... They watched the liberation of Cherbourg... took the cheers and kisses of frenzied Parisians... and gaped as the 17th A/B flew over to secure a bridgehead on the lower Rhine. One detachment got as far as Pollwitz, a few miles from Czechoslovakia.*
>
> *Almost any man in this peripatetic unit can toast in six different languages and talk knowingly of the ETO campaign from the beaches to the Elbe.*[11]

The Ghost Army remained classified until the 1980s. Fred Fox died in 1981.

* * *

I love the story of Captain Fred Fox and the Ghost Army for obvious reasons. It's a mind-blowing tale that truly deserves to be brought to the big screen. The very existence of this unit is a testament to the incredible ingenuity and creativity of the United States military. Beyond the fascinating dynamics of the story itself, the Ghost Army exemplifies why our military is the greatest on earth. This unit wasn't about brute force but about using creativity and wild imagination to achieve a common goal.

Fred Fox enjoyed an audience, but he knew that ultimately, we're performing for an Audience of One. The Bible says that every Christian also enjoys the invisible support of a heavenly "cloud of witnesses," cheering us on like we're in a race. Most members of the Ghost Army never received earthly rewards for their efforts. One of them, when asked by his family what he did during the war, would cryptically respond, "I blew up tanks," without mentioning that the tanks were inflatable![12]

Ultimately, however, everyone got to be in on the inside joke. In 2024, the remaining seven members of the unit received a Congressional Gold Medal.

At the ceremony, Fred's son, the Reverend Donald Fox, prayed to bless the proceedings. "Here we are assembled around the Statue of Freedom surrounded by a great cloud of witnesses," he said. "We thank you, God, that the men of the Ghost Army are being recognized as soldiers who made a huge contribution to winning World War II in Europe without hardly ever firing a gun. We thank you for the way that these 1,100 individuals with their creative courage represent the best in our nation, one nation, under God, indivisible."[13]

I love the history of the United States military. I love reading stories about the heroic deeds and valor of those who came before. But what many don't realize is that, like virtually every other core pillar of our nation, the military was founded on

Judeo-Christian values. Every branch of the U.S. military is deeply steeped in Christian teachings. The core principles of the U.S. Army—loyalty, duty, respect, selfless service, honor, integrity, and personal courage—aren't just words; they are the foundation that has shaped our soldiers and our military since the very beginning.

These values are not simply abstract ideals but are rooted in biblical teachings that emphasize the inherent worth of every individual and the importance of serving a purpose greater than oneself. For generations, American soldiers have been guided by these principles, carrying with them the belief that their service is not just a duty to their country but a moral obligation to uphold justice and freedom.

At its core, the U.S. military is not just a fighting force; it is a guardian of the ideals that have defined America since its inception. These ideals promote justice, mercy, and humility before a higher power. John 15:13 (KJV) reads, "Greater love hath no man than this, that a man lay down his life for his friends." A placard bearing this quote is prominently displayed at the entrance of the West Point Cadet Chapel. It serves as a solemn reminder of the ultimate sacrifice many soldiers make in service to their country.

When young men or women join the military, they are taught not just to follow orders but to serve with honor, protecting the innocent and upholding the sanctity of human life. This moral framework has been a guiding light in times of peace and war, shaping our military into more than just an instrument of power—it is a force for good in the world.

There's a common phrase that reads, "To a man with a hammer, everything looks like a nail."

The metaphor suggests that a person who only knows how

to use a hammer will treat all problems as though they can be solved by hammering instead of considering other tools or solutions. It highlights the importance of flexibility, critical thinking, and being open to different approaches when solving problems.

Fred Fox had many more tools besides a hammer. The men who fought in the Ghost Army were not your typical warriors. They were artists and dreamers. What I love about this story is that it was filled with men who loved God. The men of the Ghost Army used their gifts in service of a higher calling. Even such a massive force as the United States military was able to step back and tap into the vision of Fred Fox and others who reimagined the battle and fought not with guns and bombs but with inflatable tanks and speakers!

Lessons Learned

CREATIVITY AND INGENUITY CAN BE POWERFUL TOOLS FOR ACHIEVING GOALS. The story of the Ghost Army perfectly shows how the United States military used deception, rather than brute force, to outsmart the enemy. Through inflatable tanks, fake buildings, and sound effects, they created an illusion that misled the German forces. One of the biggest tools we have is the ability to think outside the box. When facing what looks to be an impossible challenge, using creative strategies can sometimes achieve what sheer strength cannot.

EXCELLENCE IS A BETTER MOTIVATOR THAN ATTENTION. Captain Fred Fox and his team may not have received the recognition they deserved in life, but this didn't stop them from putting on the best performance they possibly could. Their audience was bigger than the Germans. They knew that God sees every job done well and honors it in the end. The Ghost Army's efforts were not for personal glory but to save lives by diverting German attention away from the real Allied forces. By creating this diversion, they reduced casualties and played a critical role in advancing the Allied cause. Serving a cause bigger than oneself, even in unseen ways, can have far-reaching effects that will echo into eternity.

FAITH AND PURPOSE CAN STRENGTHEN RESOLVE. Throughout their mission, the members of the Ghost Army, including Captain Fox, leaned on their faith, praying together before their operations. This faith provided them with the courage to carry out their duties, even in the face of immense risk. Having a deeper sense of purpose, whether spiritual or moral, can give people the strength to persevere in the most challenging circumstances.

Chapter 5

CHARLES AND MARGARET KAIROUZ

Echoes into Eternity

Just after the turn of the twentieth century, around 1905, young Margaret Simon boarded a ship with her family, leaving behind the familiar hills of Becheri, Lebanon. Becheri was a long-time refuge for Christians, and since Aramaic had endured as a liturgical language well into the 1800s, the people of Margaret's town spoke with a distinctive accent—an accent inflected with the sound of the language Jesus spoke, two thousand years before. Becheri was deep in the Kadisha Valley. "Kadisha" meant "holy" in Aramaic. Margaret had felt an ache in her soul as she watched the familiar pale cream-and-orange buildings disappear behind her, vanishing down the long cliffs of the Holy Valley.

The family sailed toward the promise of America, the "land of the free," braving the vast Atlantic with little more than hope in their hearts. Their journey ended in the bustling, industrial city of Toledo, Ohio, where they settled among other immigrant families, trying to carve out a new life. In the cold foreignness of a new world, bereft of her valley, her people, her language, Margaret wondered, would God have followed her over the sea?

Margaret's early years in America remain largely a mystery, but by the time she was a teenager, she had played an unexpected part in the infamous story of her older brother, Tonoose.

Tonoose had fallen deeply in love, which wasn't unusual—except for one detail: the girl he loved had already been promised to another man, Shaheed, back in Lebanon. Arranged marriages were considered unbreakable, especially for something as transient as the shallow love of a teenager. But, Tonoose reasoned, Shaheed was on the other side of the world. As Tonoose Simon—who by now was calling himself "Tony"—romanced Julia Saad, he thought, *This is a new world, with new ways. Why not embrace this world's tradition of love matches?*

Of course, this was all well and good, right up until word came that Shaheed wasn't on the other side of the world at all—he was crossing the ocean. He was going to be in Toledo the very next day.

For Tony, the thought of losing Julia was unbearable. With reckless abandon, he convinced his beloved to elope with him.

Back in Lebanon, such an act would have ignited a blood feud. The history books—and whispered family lore—were filled with tales of vengeance, families wiped out in honor-fueled battles, not unlike the Hatfields and McCoys. When Shaheed arrived and learned what had happened, tension gripped the Simon and Saad households like a vise. Nineteen-year-old Shaheed was furious, raging for days to his father about the broken trust. His father, a patriarch in the community, realized that the only way to head off violence was to get his son—a well-educated man whose good sense would, he hoped, overcome his fury—to talk to the family of his former betrothed.

So they arranged a meeting. As Shaheed entered the Simon home, his face was heavy with heartbreak and anger; he was ready to demand restitution or at least closure. But then something unexpected happened. With quiet dignity, he announced that there would be no feud. "I forgive you," he said to Tony's mother, making it clear that he would not be carrying out the feud. The family exhaled in relief.

It was then that Margaret entered the room, her voice cutting through the weight of the moment. "Would you like a glass of water?" she asked.

Perhaps it was her kindness, or perhaps it was fate, but Shaheed looked at Margaret and saw his future. In later years, he would speak of that moment as when he truly fell in love. Suddenly, losing Julia wasn't such a problem.

Shaheed and Margaret married and began a life that was as difficult as it was hopeful. In those early years, Shaheed worked tirelessly—when he wasn't laboring in a factory, he was scavenging alleys for scraps to sell or tending a church garden. It wasn't until he had saved enough for a horse and wagon that things began to improve. With these tools, he became a traveling peddler, selling dry goods and kitchenware to make ends meet.

Margaret, meanwhile, became a mother at just fifteen. Her first child was followed in quick succession by three more. For years, the family traveled with Shaheed, sleeping in fields and cooking over open campfires as he sold his wares. But by the time Margaret was pregnant with her fifth child, she had had enough. "I need a home," she told her husband. And so, they bought a small horse farm in Deerfield, Michigan.

It was there that Muzyad, their fifth child, was born. Sensing the challenges their children might face with traditional Lebanese names, Shaheed and Margaret soon changed Muzyad's name to Amos. In fact, they changed all of their boys' names to more traditional "American-sounding" names. And Shaheed changed his name to Charles. The family grew to include ten children in total—nine boys and one girl.

The defining moment of Margaret's life came when Amos was just six months old. One night as the baby slept in his crib, a rat crawled in and bit his tiny hand. His screams pierced the night, and Margaret and Charles rushed him to the hospital. But in 1912, medicine could do little for rat-bite fever. Amos burned with a relentless fever, and the doctors sent him home, offering no hope.

Margaret refused to accept this. With her baby's life hanging by a thread, she knelt on the floor and prayed. Her words were raw and desperate:

"Please, God, spare him. If you do, I vow to beg for pennies door-to-door for a whole year to give to the poor. Spare my baby. Please, God, spare my baby."

Against all odds, Amos survived. True to her word, Margaret spent the next year fulfilling her vow. Each morning, she rode the streetcar to the end of the line, and from there, she walked back, knocking on doors. With her thick Middle Eastern accent, she would plead, "Please give pennies to the poor. I promised God. Please."

Some doors were slammed in her face, but many were opened. People gave her the pennies she requested so humbly, each one a testament to her faith and determination.

Amos's father, Charles, was stern and practical, rarely displaying his emotions. The first time his children saw him pray was the night Amos's fever broke. That moment of vulnerability, coupled with Margaret's devotion, strengthened the faith of the entire family.

Margaret never learned to read or write, and her accent marked her as an outsider, even among people who worshipped the son of God, who had the same accent. Yet she embodied the essence of perseverance, humility, and faith. Her daily treks for pennies became a family legend; a story retold to inspire her children and grandchildren.

The story of Charles and Margaret, like all of our stories, is multigenerational. It did not start with them, nor did it end with them. Their choices, sacrifices, and prayers were never just about them. Charles and Margaret understood that their actions and prayers would echo into eternity. It was their fifth child, Amos, who grew up in the suburbs of Toledo, Ohio, who would go on to change the face of our nation and impact hundreds of thousands of lives. It was Amos who would not simply further his parents' dreams but shatter every glass ceiling in the process.

From a very young age, Amos sold newspapers, shined shoes, and worked as a delivery boy. He grew up in an atmosphere of great faith. His mother especially loved God and prayed with the children daily. He recalled, "My mom... was the gentlest, kindest, most honest, loving person I have ever known... brilliant—in her plain, everyday, horse-sense way. Also, she had a faith in God I've never seen matched anywhere."[14]

Amos wanted to aim high to repay his parents for their loving care. He decided to become a doctor. But after facing rejection from multiple medical schools due to his inability to pay tuition, he was eventually forced to abandon his dream.

Distraught and feeling like a failure, Amos stepped back and assessed his life. *What am I good at?* The thought consumed him. *What comes naturally to me? What do I want to do with my life?* You see, unlike his parents, who didn't really have a choice, Amos did. Because of the sacrifices of Charles and Margaret, Amos had the luxury of dreaming daring dreams. Charles and Margaret's life didn't have any margins. They had dreams, but they also had five kids to feed and shelter. They did all they could to survive and to provide for their children. They lived beautiful and fulfilled lives, but taking a breath and stepping back to dream about potential opportunities was not an option for them. It was their great sacrifice that provided their children with this opportunity. The opportunity to dream. The opportunity to try new things. The opportunity to fail miserably and get back up to try again.

This is exactly what Amos did. After "failing" to become a doctor, he turned his attention to a career in entertainment. At first, his parents were against the idea. Still, over time, it became clear that Amos was approaching this new career with the same work ethic and conviction that had characterized his previous endeavors, and he eventually earned their support.

After performing in several clubs, Amos decided that his name, Amos Muzyad Yaqoob Kairouz, was still too foreign-sounding for local audiences, so he officially changed it to Danny Thomas, using the names of two of his brothers. He performed in small clubs and theaters for a few years, honing his talents as a stand-up comedian. Even so, he never found real success. As more years passed, Danny fell in love with a woman who was working as a singer at one of the nightclubs where he performed. Her name was Rose Marie, and not long after, they were married. Even more years passed, and still, Danny couldn't even afford to get Rose nice clothes—and now she was pregnant with their first child, Margaret, who'd eventually be nicknamed Marlo.

One night, Danny watched Bob Hope perform at a Detroit club where he also worked, and was astonished to observe "how a real pro can captivate an audience." Danny made mental notes, but he felt discouraged when he couldn't retain his audience over the coming days and weeks. Eventually, he slipped into a deep depression.

Finally, when he was desperate and had hit rock bottom, something surprising happened. One night after his set, he was sitting at the bar drowning his sorrows, only to see a man stagger in, jovially drunk—or so it seemed. The man walked right up to Danny, happily babbling about St. Jude and how everyone should know his name. Danny rolled his eyes. A drunken, religious nut! He stood to leave.

But the man grabbed his shoulder. "You think I'm drunk?" he said, and paused for a moment. "Well, I *am* drunk. But I know what I'm saying. It's just that I'm not saying it so good right now."

Danny stayed and listened to the man's dramatic tale. His wife had been dying of terminal cancer of the uterus, and in his desperation, thinking of St. Jude—the patron saint of lost causes—he'd prayed that God would heal his wife, vowing that in return, he would tell everyone about St. Jude, and how no cause is ever lost.

The man left soon after, but Danny found himself oddly moved by his tale. The next day, he went to church, even though it was the middle of the week.

He knelt and prayed a prayer of desperation. It was a simple prayer. "Help me find my way in life, and I will build you a shrine," he promised. He explained that he felt hopeless and that even though—he felt embarrassed to admit—it wasn't a life-or-death situation, he truly felt called into show business, and he wanted to succeed in it. Surely, he wondered, God didn't care about these little things—just life, death, world peace.

But he underestimated God.

Soon afterward, on a gut feeling, he took a solo trip to Chicago, based on nothing but the sense that he should look for work in the big time—and one connection, with a man who worked in radio. As the city's skyline came into view, Danny felt a wave of panic strike him and he pulled over, going into a church.

"I felt a sudden surge of something I can't explain," he wrote later. "It wasn't mystical or supernatural. But my brain became filled with the overwhelming thought: 'Oh, ye of little faith!'"

He steeled himself to go on.

His friend in radio was thrilled to see him, and put him to work as a character actor.[15]

After this, the tides shifted for Danny. He was offered lead roles on successful radio shows and eventually starred in his own television series, *The Danny Thomas Show*, which was an immense success and ran for eleven seasons.

Later, he actually became friends with Bob Hope, who found Danny's faith so obvious he used to kid him. "Danny Thomas is so religious that he gets stopped by the highway patrol because he has stained glass windows in his car," he'd joke.

Thomas found himself rubbing shoulders with celebrities from Dean Martin to Magic Johnson and eventually even presidents. Ronald Reagan once quipped, "I was a little embarrassed when I first came to the White House and they played 'Hail to the Chief' when I entered the room—until I found out that when Danny Thomas walks in, they play Handel's *Messiah*."[16]

* * *

I love Danny's story because it epitomizes the American Dream. The prayers and sacrifice of his parents paved the way for Danny to achieve greatness. And if this was where Danny's story ended, I would still love it! Yet not a day went by that Danny didn't reflect on the desperate prayer he had once made: "Help me find my way in life, and I will build you a shrine."

As the years passed, Danny became consumed by a powerful idea. The memory of his mother going door-to-door, begging for pennies for an entire year, never left his mind. She had made a vow to God, and it didn't matter how humiliated she felt, how exhausted she became, or how many doors were slammed in her face—she kept that promise, no matter what. Though Danny had failed to become a doctor, he began to wonder: *What if I could create something even greater? What if I could build a hospital that was entirely free?* Many of you are likely familiar with St. Jude Children's Research Hospital. This extraordinary institution provides treatment to children at no cost to their families, covering all aspects of care, including travel, housing, and food. Its mission is simple but profound: to ensure that no family ever receives a bill from St. Jude, allowing them to focus solely on helping their child live and thrive.

Danny Thomas did indeed live up to his promise. In 1962, he opened St. Jude. An entire book could and should be written about all the incredible science, innovation, and revolutionary treatments that have come out of the hospital. When St. Jude opened, the survival rate for ALL (acute lymphoblastic leukemia), the most common form of childhood cancer, was around 4 percent. Today, the survival rate is 94 percent, thanks to research and treatment protocols developed at St. Jude. The overall survival rate for childhood cancer has increased from 20 percent to more than 80 percent since St. Jude opened, reflecting the hospital's contributions to research and treatment.

Thousands of children are treated every year, and countless lives have been saved. Billions of dollars have been spent on treatment, research, and support services at St. Jude Children's Research Hospital, reflecting the institution's unwavering commitment to advancing cures and providing comprehensive, no-cost care to children with catastrophic diseases.

I started this chapter with the story of Danny Thomas's parents for a reason. Danny's mother, Margaret, despite the obscurity of her life from the perspective of history, yielded a mighty legacy in the light of eternity. Her faithful care and instruction of her son Danny planted in his heart the faith that God made grow. That faith motivated the care of hundreds of needy children. It's nice to be a Danny Thomas, a popular comedian whose work was lauded by his peers and seen around the nation, but we should aspire just as strongly to be a quietly faithful servant in the tradition of his mother. May our actions today echo into eternity. As my friend Pastor Mark Batterson loves to say, "Prayers don't have a shelf life." The prayers of my grandmama and my mama are being answered today. Their fervent prayers are being answered in the life of my nephew, Ben. The prayers of Charles and Margaret are still being answered daily at St. Jude!

The journey that led to the creation of St. Jude Children's Research Hospital is nothing short of miraculous—a story that could unfold only in the United States of America. Similarly, the narrative of our healthcare system is a tapestry of faith stories. Long before Danny Thomas envisioned St. Jude, countless men and women of faith were laying the foundation, forging the path that would eventually shape our nation's healthcare system into what it is today.

Like St. Jude, our healthcare system and hospitals were founded on Judeo-Christian principles. Clara Barton, known as the "Angel of the Battlefield," was a devout Christian and humanitarian. She founded the American Red Cross in 1881. Dr. Daniel Hale Williams, an African American surgeon and devout Christian, founded Provident Hospital in Chicago in 1891. Mother Frances Cabrini, a Catholic nun and the first U.S. citizen to be canonized as a saint, founded the Missionary Sisters of the Sacred Heart of Jesus in 1880. Under her leadership, the order established sixty-seven institutions, including hospitals, orphanages, and schools across the United States, focusing on providing healthcare and education to immigrants and the poor.

I could go on for hundreds of pages. The list of men and women of faith and their contributions to our healthcare system in America would be long enough to fill a library. While I chose to tell the story of Danny Thomas, the stories of any of the others mentioned above could easily have been highlighted for their profound impact. The best parts of the U.S. healthcare system are deeply rooted in Judeo-Christian principles. Our country has thrived because every major institution, every pillar, and every cornerstone of our foundation was built on biblical principles.

Danny knew the story of his parents leaving Lebanon. He knew the prayers that were prayed over them before they stepped foot on that ship. "May our actions today echo into eternity." The prayers and actions of Danny Thomas and the prayers and actions of Charles and Margaret—perseverance, hard work, determination, and prayer—continue to echo into eternity. As long as biblical principles guide us, the decisions we make today and the sacrifices we make tomorrow will echo into eternity. It is men and women guided by their faith who have changed the face of this nation!

Lessons Learned

FAITH ECHOES ACROSS GENERATIONS. The story of Charles and Margaret demonstrates how the seeds we plant will flourish eventually, even if it's not in our own lives but in the lives of our descendants.

DON'T ASSUME YOU KNOW WHAT GOD HAS NEXT FOR YOU. Danny often felt his troubles were impossible to overcome, but when he prayed, he was hoping that his gloomy outlook was wrong. And, sure enough, his prayers were answered!

THE AMERICAN DREAM IS ABOUT MORE THAN JUST EFFORT. Every hard thing we do is enabled by the grace that God has shown us. Danny recognized that despite all his own talent and hard work, he had to start by being thankful to God, who gave him those gifts.

Chapter 6

LOUIDA WARE

Live in the Light of Resurrection

Charleston, South Carolina

1933

In the predawn hours, before the first light dared to graze the eastern horizon, Louida Ware stepped out of her humble apartment to embark on her almost two-mile journey. As a Black woman in the early 1940s, Louida had limited opportunities. Like many other African American women in South Carolina, Louida worked in the homes of wealthy white families in Charleston, which she hiked to each day. The people she worked for referred to her as their "domestic servant," and if they spoke to her personally, they called her "girl." She doubted if any of her employers knew her real name.

Louida spent her days either cleaning houses or working as a "mammy," a surrogate mother to children not her own. These were the primary jobs available for a young Black woman in those days. Yet Louida was different than many of her friends: Though her life seemed constrained by a preordained narrative, her imagination ran wild. Louida harbored a silent conviction that she was destined for more.

Though she wouldn't tell a soul for many years, Louida's long-held dream was to become a nurse. As she changed linens in the homes she cleaned, she envisioned herself in a hospital room instead. She realized that this was laughable. Her eighth-grade education enabled her to read, write, and understand basic math, but she was trained for little else.

A limited education was just one of many barriers facing Louida in South Carolina in 1944. In those days, there were a few African American nurses in the United States, but they were absolutely the exceptions to the rule.

Louida's work in the homes of her wealthy white employers provided her with a front-row view of a world completely out of reach. Her dream was an undercurrent that carried her through every scrub, sweep, and polish. Every day as she worked, she imagined herself at the hospital wearing a crisp white nurse's uniform and cap and stepping into a patient's room to offer comfort. Louida could see it clearly in her mind's eye. This was her calling in life!

Louida fully understood that she was living in an unjust world, yet still, she imagined the world as it could be, as it should be! As the years passed, the world began to change. Jim Crow laws were still in full force in the 1940s, creating separate and unequal circumstances for African American men, women, and children. Blacks and whites were still divided in schools, on transportation, in housing, and even in the military. Even so, the winds of change were stirring, and the seeds of the Civil Rights Movement were being planted.

Over time, societal barriers started to crack, giving way to opportunities. Louida met a man and fell in love. It did not take long for them to get married and start a family. All the while, Louida never lost sight of her dream. Her always wild and active imagination was clear to everyone around her. Her dreams remained outrageous.

Louida became a mother of six kids, many of whom inherited her bold personality and vivid imagination. Doretha joined the army and traveled the world serving her country. Frances embodied her mother's dream: She became a nurse's assistant and worked for fifty years at Bon Secours St. Francis Hospital in Charleston, South Carolina. In fact, she retired just a year or so before I wrote these words.

Frances would have two boys of her own. One would retire from the army as a command sergeant major. The second would go into public service and eventually run for president of the United States. In case you hadn't guessed it yet, Louida was my grandmama.

I wish I could tell you that her dream of becoming a nurse came true. I cannot. In the same way, I cannot tell you that the Civil Rights Movement changed the country overnight. It did not. Dreams have a tendency to play out over time. In retrospect, change is swift and unstoppable, but when you live it daily, progress is—at best—slow and unsteady. In the midst of the struggle, change can feel a million miles away, and immovable mountains are, in fact, immovable... at least for a time.

Grandmama Louida's dream of becoming a nurse may not have materialized. Still, her spirit of care and service permeated our family, inspiring us to strive for greatness in our own ways. Her faith, prayers, and relentless imagination instilled in us a sense of strength and resilience. She taught us that the true power of dreams lies not in their fulfillment but in their ability to propel us forward, shape our character, and guide our actions with unwavering faith and determination.

Despite having only an eighth-grade education, Grandmama accomplished an incredible amount in her life. My grandaddy, who had only a third-grade education and never learned to read or write, relied on her to manage the family finances. Grandmama looked after half the community. Her house was a sanctuary where anyone in need could find a helping hand and a loving embrace. She spent countless hours at church, praying with and for people, embodying a love that knew no bounds.

Yes, there was injustice in the world that directly limited the trajectory of her life. No, it was not fair. But Grandmama Louida was not a victim. She was a hero, a champion of her time. While victims see everything wrong with the world, overcomers like my grandmama set their sights higher. They forge a path forward despite the obstacles.

I tell the story of Grandmama because I believe her life is a road map for us. The way forward for our country is not shrouded in secrecy. The road is not unknown. It's not like we are navigating uncharted territory. The answer is simple. We must play the hand we've been dealt. Rather than just complaining about injustice or unfairness, we must forge a path forward with courage, imagination, and unwavering faith.

I believe dreams have a throughline that spans generations. Unfulfilled dreams are not necessarily "no"; they are often "not yet." Grandmama Louida's dreams were not wasted; they laid the foundation for the aspirations of her children and grandchildren. Even if she couldn't realize it herself, her vision of a better future provided the groundwork for future achievements.

In a faithless generation, dreams that don't have an immediate or personal realization are wasted. If there is nothing but this material world, then our lives have meaning only in the current gratification of our desires. You can see this attitude everywhere. But even atheists should be able to recognize that an imagination that lives in the light of the resurrection ends up making a better world for everyone. Being aware that we look forward to a life beyond this one, where spiritual treasures will compensate us for lacking or deferring worldly ones, makes us truly free to live with courageous dreams and apply long-term thinking to the problems we face. Recognizing that God made us to "be fruitful and multiply" and to give of ourselves for others provides an incredible engine for progress.

Looking back through American history, we can see the effect of this Christian imagination. One of the definitive events in American history was our first president's giving up his own power willingly, handing the baton to the next generation, an act without parallel in human history, prompting King George III to call him "the greatest character of the age."[17] Washington was able to do this because he understood that this life isn't all we're promised. Even though he had no children of his own, he understood the principle of yielding our future into God's hands, exactly as my grandmother Louida did.

Our nation also has a throughline. The road map established by our Founding Fathers—through their prayers, faith, sacrifices, and wild imagination—continues to play out today. The prayers and dreams of previous generations are being answered in ways they might not have envisioned. Grandmama Louida's story is a microcosm of what is happening throughout our nation and what has been happening throughout our history.

What one generation envisions, the next will strive to achieve. Grandmama Louida lived long enough to see how the power of her wild imagination and faith propelled her family forward. She watched as her daughters shattered glass ceilings. Although she never wore a nurse's uniform and cap, her daughter did, and her great-grandson became a doctor. Grandmama Louida defined victory as shifting the paradigm for future generations, a legacy my mother continued for my brother and me.

Lessons Learned

IMAGINATION HAS THE POWER TO TRANSCEND LIMITATIONS. My grandmama, despite the systemic barriers of her time, allowed her imagination to take her beyond the constraints imposed on her as a Black woman in 1930s and '40s in South Carolina. Her dream of becoming a nurse fueled her daily life. Even when external circumstances seem immovable, imagination can provide hope and direction for a better future.

YOUR DREAMS WILL SHAPE FUTURE GENERATIONS. While Louida never realized her dream of becoming a nurse, her vision inspired her children and grandchildren to pursue their own ambitions. My mama, Frances, worked as a nurse's assistant, and my brother and I accomplished even more still! Unfulfilled dreams in one generation often pave the way for future accomplishments in the next.

RESILIENCE IN THE FACE OF INJUSTICE IS ESSENTIAL FOR OVERCOMING OBSTACLES. Despite the many injustices she faced, Grandmama Louida refused to view herself as a victim. Instead, she chose to move forward with courage, faith, and determination. Grandmama Louida's unfulfilled dream was not the end but the beginning of a legacy that would manifest in her children, grandchildren, and great-grandchildren. Her belief in a better future created a foundation that her descendants built upon. This throughline of dreams is also present in our nation's history, where the aspirations of past generations continue to influence and shape the present and future.

Chapter 7

HORATIO SPAFFORD

Faith Isn't about What We Feel but What We Know

December 1, 1873, 2:00 a.m.

The howling wind whipped the snow into a blinding fury as Horatio Spafford charged through the tempest, racing down King Street. He stumbled but rose again with fierce determination and continued his frenzied pursuit. His stocking feet had long been numb, but it hardly registered in his mind. *No! Please, God, no!* echoed relentlessly in his soul.

As Horatio neared the harbor, he squinted through the raging storm. His breath caught in his throat as he saw them standing at the pier's edge, their crimson dresses whipping wildly around them. "Children!" he gasped, staggering forward. His beautiful wife, Anna, turned to face him, cradling baby Tanetta in her arms. Annie, Maggie, and Bessie stood on either side, grasping their mother tightly. The world spun as Horatio crumbled. Drained of strength, he began to crawl.

All four girls watched their father with a mixture of curiosity and sadness. Above the howling wind and his own labored breaths, Horatio heard the gentle sounds of his youngest daughter's cooing. Tears streamed down his face as he forced his limbs to move, inching ever closer.

A ferocious gust of wind shrouded his family in a flurry of ice and snow. "No!" Horatio screamed, lunging forward with arms outstretched. But as the wind subsided, his girls vanished. Deep within his tormented mind, he knew they had never truly been there. His grief had conjured the vision.

Horatio had started running because he needed to do something, anything. He'd come to the pier because it was the last place he'd seen them. But there was never any chance of saving his family. The crumpled telegram in his fist confirmed the awful truth: The girls had been dead for days. His wife's telegram, sent from the other side of the Atlantic, had delivered the news with agonizing simplicity: "Saved alone. What shall I do?"

It's difficult to imagine a parent's pain in these moments. Horatio's guilt was compounded by the fact that he'd sent his family on to Europe on the ship *Ville du Havre* and stayed behind on business. He'd weathered financial storms in his life, losing much of his investments in the Great Chicago Fire a few years before. But Horatio was a man of faith. He knew that ultimately the wealth we pile up in this life is unimportant. Preserving the lives of his family was his most important responsibility.

But now what could he do? Those lives were gone.

Unbidden, the last moment of his girls' lives played out in his mind. He could see the vision as clearly as if he had been standing on the ship's deck with them. Beautiful Anna and the girls huddled together in a loving cluster, their faces etched with fear. Maggie tried to reassure her younger sister, "It's going to be all right. God will take care of us." Suddenly, the ship lurched violently. It had been struck by another, far larger craft, and was going down fast. Annie noticed her mother straining to keep hold of baby Tanetta. She wrapped her arms around her mother's, offering help.

Later, his wife described the scene: "The dear children were so brave. They died praying. Annie said to Maggie and me just before we were swept off the steamer, 'Don't be frightened, Maggie, God will take care of us, we can trust Him; and you know, Mama, "The sea is His and He made it."' These were her last words. Maggie and Bessie prayed very sweetly."

Then they were torn apart. Horatio's wife grabbed desperately for Tanetta's little gown, and for a desperate moment it was in her hand—then the waters tore it from her. As she sank into the deep, she felt a plank rise under her, pushing her to the surface, keeping her afloat. She hit her head... and all was darkness.

Some time later, a sailor found her and lifted her from the water. When she came to, covered in crusted salt and with her dressing gown shredded by the debris, "she knew, with no need of being told, that her children were gone."[18]

Now her husband faced the same knowledge. Horatio gasped for breath, shaking violently as he reached for the family that wasn't there.

The storm in Horatio's heart would abate over time. Like the biblical Job, he would call out for God and finally receive an answer, comforting him in his grief. The lessons that he had taught in the abstract as a Sunday school teacher and evangelist would become living truth in his heart. In the immediate aftermath of the tragedy, he set himself to the practical task of journeying to meet his wife. On the ship to Europe, he found himself staring at the ocean where his children now lay. The next week he penned a letter to his sister and described his thoughts:

On Thursday last we passed over the spot where she went down, in mid-ocean, the water three miles deep. But I do not think of our dear ones there. They are safe, folded, the dear lambs, and there, before very long, shall we be too. In the meantime, thanks to God, we have an opportunity to serve and praise Him for His love and mercy to us and ours. "I will praise Him while I have my being." May we each one arise, leave all, and follow Him.

Horatio clung to God in the midst of the storm. What enabled him to do this? Within a few years of the calamity, Horatio put his own explanation into artistic expression. In his own words, he revealed what allowed him to not merely say but to know that it was well with his soul. While he later changed the wording to better fit the pattern of the poetry, Horatio's first draft attested to a God who taught him to know God's goodness and faithfulness.

When peace, like a river, attendeth my way,
When sorrows, like sea-billows, roll;
Whatever my lot, Thou hast taught me to say,
It is well, it is well, with my soul.

He knew that what God had taught him to say was also something that God taught him to know. He knew this because he looked at the cross. His "blest assurance" could exist because, he wrote, "Christ hath regarded my helpless estate, and hath shed His own blood for my soul."

* * *

America finds herself in challenging times. Many feel a sense of hopelessness. Grief for what they perceive as permanently lost is all too real. It is easy to choose pessimism and despair. Yet as C. S. Lewis wrote, "Grief is like a long valley, a winding valley where any bend may reveal a totally new landscape."

Lewis was not downplaying grief. He had a front-row seat on the realities of loss and despair. Having fought in the trenches of World War I, he experienced horrors beyond imagining. Later, he would lose his wife, the love of his life, to cancer. Yet Lewis understood that even the hell that was his grief could eventually lead to beauty if he chose to keep moving forward, to not give up. If you're feeling lost or grieving for our country, know that you are not alone. In fact, you are persevering!

The harrowing yet inspiring true story of Horatio Spafford will forever remain in my heart. Despite losing his four beautiful daughters in the tragic sinking of their ship, Horatio found the strength, faith, and courage to not only carry on but also praise his Creator from the depths of his pain in the midst of the storm. Similarly, his wife wrote of the peace she found with astonishing grace: "How thankful I am that their little lives were so early dedicated to their Master. Now he has called them to Himself. . . . If I never believed in religion before, I have had strong proof of it now. We have been so sustained, so comforted. God has sent peace in our hearts. He has answered our prayers. His will be done."[19]

I can only pray that I would have such ruthless trust.

I first read that term in Brennan Manning's book *Ruthless Trust*. Manning—who wrote numerous life-changing books on the subject of grace—emphasized that trust is a fundamental aspect of faith. Trust is not a mere belief in God's existence but a deep, abiding confidence in God's love and goodness, even in the face of uncertainty and adversity. Horatio and Anna Spafford understood ruthless trust.

Today, America finds herself weathering a storm of a different kind. Our schools are failing our children, and our porous borders are failing the entire country. Crime is at record highs, and police morale is at an all-time low. War rages on multiple fronts, with the potential for greater conflict feeling eminent—namely, the unprecedented fentanyl and drug epidemic. During the Biden administration, the DOJ was trying to imprison Biden's political rivals, a strategy that echoes into our time now. Our children's identities are under siege, and traditional family values are openly mocked. You know the list of issues as well as I do, and it continues.

I recently ran for president. The experience was the greatest honor of my life. Though I should have expected it, I am still surprised at just how much the journey changed me. The man I have evolved into today is not the man who announced his presidential bid. My last book was a memoir titled *America, a Redemption Story*. I am proud of the book and the stories I told. Every last page is brimming with stories of hope and optimism. While those two words—"hope" and "optimism"—will always define me, the process of running to become the president of the United States of America brought me face-to-face with a new word: "reckoning."

While traveling from state to state, knocking on doors, and

meeting so many of my fellow citizens, I could not have been more proud to be an American. I met countless men and women who care immensely for this great country. I met thousands of Americans who wake up and go to work daily, who love their spouses and sacrifice for their children. These are the people who are building our great nation. These are the men and women who personify greatness.

As I crisscrossed the country, I began to understand that the despair and pessimism that so many feel today is enormous. After spending numerous months hearing the stories of what so many in this great nation are facing, hearing their heartbreak and fears firsthand, I have to be honest: I began to feel a deep sense of righteous indignation!

Hope and optimism are paramount. I will never apologize for choosing hope over despair and will always choose optimism in the face of pessimism. The very definition of despair is when you can see no possibility of improving a given situation. Despair is the feeling of profound defeat. Pessimism is the tendency to see the worst aspect of things or believe that the worst will happen. Pessimism leads to a profound lack of hope for the future. Optimism doesn't mean ignoring the dangers and threats we face. Horatio Spafford was in a certain sense a profound realist. He could hardly deny the reality of suffering. But like Job, he also knew that God is real. It would be *unrealistic* to lose all hope given this truth. In the final line of an early version of his hymn, Horatio quoted Job, alluding to the God who "gives songs in the night" (Job 35:10).

In the final version's last line, "'Even so'—it is well with my soul," he alludes to that final promise in Scriptures' concluding lines: "Even so, come, Lord Jesus" (Revelations 22:20).

I understand the draw to despair. On virtually every front, dark forces push to influence our sons and daughters. Shameless lies are boldly shouted from the rooftops. Virtually every time I turn on the news, I see a new attack from those who seem hell-bent on tearing apart the very fabric of our nation. What is needed now is not simply to be brought together. What we need now is a bull in a china shop. And over the past year or so, I have begun feeling like that bull. Despair is disobedience for Christians.

America needs a reckoning. We must have an awakening. It is not enough to simply understand the consequences of our political and moral failures; we must take back the moral high ground! And taking it back will not be easy. This is a fight for America's heart and soul.

I tell the story of Horatio Spafford for a reason. I can think of no greater darkness than that of losing your children. The pain Horatio must have experienced is unimaginable. He must have felt an all-consuming rage against his Creator. Yet in the moment of his greatest darkness, in an act of ruthless trust, in a moment of brutal faith, Horatio fought back the only way he knew how. Though I suspect he could not have felt it in the moment, Horatio made the impossible choice to lean into the goodness of God. He made the impossible choice to praise his Creator in the midst of the storm.

When I say we need a reckoning, I mean that America is in a Horatio Spafford moment. The darkness is great, and we must stand up to it. Evil exists, and there can be no compromise with it. We are at a crossroads. Embrace the darkness and end the dream that is America, or fight tooth and nail to take back our country's soul.

I have come to believe that we are never taller than when we are on our knees. It would have been easy for Horatio to walk away and curse God. No one would have blamed him. It would have been easy for him to embrace the darkness. Despair and pessimism were the natural choice. It was impossible for Horatio to choose faith. There is no other word for it. And still, he chose it.

Like Horatio, each of us must make the impossible choice. This is the only way forward. This is the only answer to the surrounding darkness. This is the only way to take back America. And, like Horatio, we begin and end this battle on our knees in prayer before our Creator. Our battle starts with humility. I am not writing about a physical battle. I am also not simply talking about hope and optimism. The "day of reckoning" is here. The consequences of many of the laws and actions of those who seek to eliminate God from our public spaces and the decisions and policies that have been implemented must be confronted.

Now let us get on our knees and lean into God with all our strength. And then let us stand. Let us be the reckoning. Let us be the awakening America needs. We will not simply stand by and watch the fabric of America unravel. And let us remember that if we don't fight first on our knees, we are fighting in vain.

These are challenging times, without question. But I believe a new generation of men and women like Horatio Spafford will rise to take their place as beacons of light in the midst of these storms.

Lessons Learned

I believe that Horatio Spafford's life exemplifies three fundamental principles that can guide each of us through our own darkest moments.

CHOOSE WHAT YOU KNOW OVER WHAT YOU FEEL. When Horatio faced unimaginable grief after losing his daughters, he made the impossible choice to lean into his faith rather than succumb to despair. His hymn, "It Is Well with My Soul," is less about his feelings than his commitment to trust in God even when he couldn't see the way forward. That commitment is deeply grounded in his familiarity with scripture. All throughout his famous hymn are allusions to the Bible, a testament to his deep roots in God's revelation. This act of faith serves as a reminder that in times of great darkness, we can choose to trust in something greater than ourselves, drawing on the wisdom God gives us in His word.

CHANNEL GRIEF INTO CREATIVE EXPRESSION. Horatio's choice to turn his pain into art wasn't just a shapeless venting of his grief but a disciplined act of meaning-making. In the wake of his sorrow, Horatio penned words that would later inspire millions. He transformed his grief into a song of hope and resilience. Like Horatio, we can find ways to express our pain creatively, whether through writing, music, or acts of kindness. This process not only helps us heal but also creates something that can offer solace to others in their own struggles.

BUILD COMMUNITY AND SEEK SUPPORT. After the tragedies that befell his family, Horatio didn't retreat into isolation. Instead, he and his wife dedicated their lives to helping others by founding the American Colony of Jerusalem—a community dedicated to humanitarian work, providing aid to people of all faiths through schools, hospitals, and orphanages. With this act of service, they brought healing not only to those they helped but also to themselves. By serving others, we often find the strength to move beyond our own pain, discovering that healing can come through giving.

In forming the American Colony, Horatio surrounded himself with a community that shared his values and mission. This community provided him with support, reminding us that in our most challenging times, we must lean on others. Whether through family, friends, or faith communities, we can find strength in the connections we build. Together, we are stronger than we are alone.

Part II

Revival

Therefore, since we are receiving a kingdom that cannot be shaken, let us be thankful, and so worship God acceptably with reverence and awe.

—HEBREWS 12:28

Chapter 8

SAMUEL DAVIES

How Gratitude Leads to Revival

"Among the many vices that are at once universally decried, and universally practiced in the world, there is none more base or more common than INGRATITUDE," thundered Samuel Davies, regarding the packed audience with an expression firm but kind. "Ingratitude is the sin of individuals, of families, of churches, of kingdoms, and even of all mankind. The guilt of ingratitude lies heavy upon the whole race of men, though, alas! but few of them feel and lament it. I have felt it of late with unusual weight; and it is the weight of it that now extorts a discourse from me upon this subject."

Samuel had much to be thankful for. Despite suffering great loss in his life as well, he was able to make the same choice as Horatio Spafford, to believe in the storm. His faith was the spark that kindled national revival, and revival went on to revolution. In other words, his life and example are ones we should study very closely today, in our times of spiritual apathy.

Samuel knew that belief starts with prayer. His very life was an answer to prayer. His parents, David and Mary Davies, were Baptists of Welsh ancestry, living in a farming community in Delaware, one of the original thirteen colonies, in the years preceding the American Revolution. Born in 1723, Samuel was named after the biblical prophet. As an adult, he would refer to himself as "a son of prayer," for his mother had prayed to the Lord for a son, just as Samuel's mother did in the Bible. "I was blessed with a mother whom I might account, without filial vanity or partiality, one of the most eminent saints I ever knew upon earth," Samuel later wrote. "The most important blessings of my life I have looked upon as immediate answers to the prayers of a pious mother."[20]

His parents dedicated him to God even before he was born.

Although Samuel's parents were almost entirely uneducated, they held a deep appreciation for the value of education. His father was a man "of ordinary talents" known to live "with great plainness and simplicity," but his mother was more ambitious. During the early eighteenth century, most children's education was informal—often, for boys, occurring through apprenticeships. Formal schooling was scarce and typically reserved for the wealthy. Despite their limitations, Samuel's parents recognized that education was a pathway to greater opportunities. His mother put him under the tutelage of a local reverend, but this was to come to an end around his tenth birthday, when his mother was excommunicated from her local congregation for what they perceived as a violation of their trust: She'd been carrying stories of their church to the local Presbyterian sect.

This may seem like an overreaction on the part of her church, but some history is helpful here. In those days, the church was regulated by the British government. The Anglican church was wary of any dissenting congregations that sprang up among the people, and tended to frown on its members being seduced away by nonconformist ministers. While Mary Davies was cast out of a Baptist congregation, the incident underlines how seriously churches took their distinctions—a theme that would eventually become very important for her son. It's likely that Mary was already starting to question theology on her own, and study scripture to come to her own conclusions, which led her to Presbyterianism.

Following these events, she sent Samuel to a local classical school to complete his education. His professor and pastor (for in those days, teaching and preaching often went hand in hand), the Reverend William Robinson, was struck by the young boy's quick grasp of knowledge. Samuel didn't take an unusual interest in religion at first, but when he was twelve, he started to be thoughtful and anxious about his eternal future, and to pray a "secret prayer" at night, worried that he would "die before morning." For a long time, Samuel struggled to suppress this scrupulosity and fear. How could God truly love someone as ungrateful and unworthy as he was? But gradually, he felt the peace and assurance of God's grace settle in his heart, and with it, overwhelming gratitude.

This early dedication to education and faith laid the foundation for the rest of his life. In his early twenties, Samuel Davies was praying when he heard the still, small voice of the Holy Spirit calling him into full-time ministry. It was 1745, and the thirteen U.S. colonies were in the midst of what would eventually become known as our nation's First Great Awakening.

The Great Awakening was a period of intense religious revival that swept through the American colonies in the 1730s and

'40s. This movement was characterized by powerful preaching that sought to rekindle a deep and intimate relationship with God. Central figures like Jonathan Edwards and George Whitefield delivered sermons emphasizing personal repentance and a direct, emotional connection with the Holy Spirit, challenging the formalism and complacency of established churches.

When Samuel preached about a personal and loving relationship with God, it was revolutionary. It contrasted sharply with the prevailing religious norms that emphasized fear, obedience, and the notion of an unapproachable deity. Samuel's belief in a God who was intimately involved in his life and who delighted in his presence infused every sermon with warmth and authenticity. Samuel's relationship with God was not just about duty or fear but about love, intimacy, and mutual delight. This belief became a cornerstone of his ministry, offering a transformative vision of faith that emphasized God's care and interest in each individual.

While young Samuel may have felt the calling to seek his future as a minister, he would need a theological education. With little but the clothes on his back, he traveled to Pennsylvania to attend a "log college," as the early Presbyterian schools of theology were termed.[21]

His life was one of frequent worry and financial stress. Back home, Samuel's mother and father scrimped and saved, doing their best to send money to support their son's studies, but from day to day, he struggled to balance his work with the pressure of poverty.

Little did Samuel know that help was about to arrive from an unexpected source. His old pastor, William Robinson, had been traveling and evangelizing in Virginia and happened to pass through a county experiencing a revival.

In Hanover County, a rich planter had stumbled on a few leaves of a theological book, and the message in them had struck him so deeply that he wouldn't rest until he had the full book. Around the same time, a bricklayer discovered the sermons of George Whitefield. The message was so powerful that crowds would appear to listen to the man read them. These influential men set out to spread the peace they'd found, and discovered a deep hunger in the people of Virginia for the word of God.

This revival was not looked upon with a friendly eye by the established church. People were frequently fined for missing church in order to go to these sermon readings. The Virginia lieutenant governor sneered at "ministers under the pretended influence of... fanatical and enthusiastic knowledge."[22]

When Robinson arrived, his preaching fanned the flames of revival still higher, which couldn't have endeared him to the authorities.

When his visit was over and he planned to head back home to Delaware, the people of Hanover County tried to give him a large monetary gift. He resisted, pointing out that it would make his motives look impure if he took the money, but he found the people hard to persuade. Finally, he hit on a solution.

He exclaimed, "I will tell you what must be done with the money. There is a very promising young man, now studying divinity at the North, whose parents are very hard pressed, and find great difficulties in supporting him at his studies. I will take this money, and it shall be given to help him through. And when he is licensed, he shall come and be your preacher."[23]

This Samuel did, and his sermons contributed to a spiritual revival that would forever shape the religious, moral, and political landscape of the American colonies. He preached with a fervor that electrified congregations. His sermons were beautifully constructed, elegant pieces of rhetoric, delivered with passion and earnestness. As much as he thundered about the guilt of mankind, he also poured into the wounds the healing power of grace.

And he spoke to such matters with true experience, for while still a young man, he suffered a tremendous loss. He lost his wife and unborn son to a miscarriage in 1747. Since he had a bad case of tuberculosis around the same time, he also felt that his own death was imminent, and he fell into a deep gloom. He ended up recovering, but the experience changed him. He threw himself with renewed urgency into preaching because of his awareness of how fleeting and precious life was.[24]

For Samuel, blessed with loving parents and a hard-won education, and despite the trials of grief, ingratitude was a mighty sin. In one particularly rousing sermon, he drew the hearers' attention to the overflowing blessings of God.

Let us acknowledge the light of yonder sun, the breath that now heaves our lungs, and fans the vital flame, the growing plenty that is now bursting its way through the clods of earth, the water that bubbles up in springs, that flows in streams and rivers, or rolls at large in the ocean; let us own, I say, that all these are the bounties of his hand, who supplies with good the various ranks of being, as high as the most exalted angel, and as low as the young ravens, and the grass of the field.

He continued to highlight how hypocritical human beings are in withholding our prayers of gratitude from a loving God. "How do you resent it, if one whom you have deeply obliged should prove ungrateful, and abuse you?" he pointed out. "But it is impossible any one of your fellow-creatures should be guilty of such enormous ingratitude towards you as you are guilty of towards God; because it is impossible that any one of them should be as strongly obliged to you as you are to him!"

It's hard for modern secular people to understand the concept of worship. When God demands that we worship Him, isn't it just a sign that God is thin-skinned and proud? Who among us would go around demanding compliments without seeming vain? This is a wrongheaded way of looking at it. Samuel understood that, at base, when God demands worship, He's demanding not flattery but the appropriate gratitude for his role in our lives. When our parents ask that we show them respect, it's not because they're proud; it's because this is the proper response to how much they do to keep us on the straight and narrow. Think about how you feel when you see a little kid talk back to a patient parent. You feel offended, and rightly so! Think about how you'd feel if you saw a great artist unveil her masterpiece only to be met with indifference. We'd feel the lack of praise like it was a drought in the planting season.

Yet how often do we feel guilty for our indifference to God's blessings? We'll raise the roof if someone ignores our contribution to a project but sleepwalk through our daily devotionals, taking for granted the salvation God won at the loss of his own life. But Samuel also knew that there was no point in piling up burdens on a person's conscience without also emphasizing the depths of God's mercy.

"His love to you is an unbounded ocean, that spreads over eternity, and makes it, as it were, the channel of the ocean of your happiness," he said. "What is all the profession of kings to their favorites, what are all the benefactions of creatures, nay, what are all the bounties of the divine hand itself within the compass of time when compared to these astonishing, unparalleled, immortal, infinite, God-like favors? They all dwindle into obscurity, like the stars of night in the blaze of noon!"

Like his parents, Samuel Davies was a passionate advocate for education, believing a well-informed public was essential for the health of the church and society. He established several schools in Virginia, providing instruction not only in religious subjects but also in classical languages, philosophy, and science. These schools helped elevate the colonies' intellectual life and prepared a new generation of leaders. It is safe to say that the echoes of Samuel's prayers and actions are still being felt today.

In one of his more famous sermons, Samuel stood in a room filled to bursting. The rise and fall of his voice held the congregation spellbound as he preached a storm. "I must repeat it again, that the Holy Spirit is the only effectual reformer of the world! It is He alone who can effectually 'reprove the world of sin.' If He is absent—legislators may make laws against crime; philosophers may reason against vice; ministers may preach against sin; conscience may remonstrate against evil; the divine law may prescribe and threaten hell; the gospel may invite and allure to heaven, but all will be in vain! The strongest arguments, the most melting entreaties, the most alarming denunciations from God and man, enforced with the highest authority, or the most compassionate tears—all will have no effect—all will not effectually reclaim one sinner, nor gain one sincere convert to righteousness!"

The power and passion of these words resonated deeply with those who heard them, stirring hearts and minds. The idea of a close and personal relationship with the Holy Spirit swept the colonies like wildfire. This message resonated powerfully with countless colonists seeking more than the ritualistic and formalistic religion they had known. Revival meetings became places where individuals could publicly confess their sins, express their faith, and feel a real sense of personal connection to God. The focus on personal religious experience democratized religious life, allowing laypeople to play a more active role in their spiritual journey. This shift had profound effects on American religion, leading to the growth of new denominations and fostering a sense of religious equality that would shape the nation's future.

Part of Samuel's brilliance was that he knew how to wisely interact with the authorities in the established church. While he never compromised with them, he took care to reassure the bishop of London, for instance, that his goal was not to steal away Anglican parishioners but to convert the many lost souls who he perceived were not being sought by an established minister. Authentic converts were all he desired, he said, claiming, "I would rather that men were made members of the church triumphant in the regions of bliss by the preaching of a minister of the Church of England, than that they should remain unconverted in a Presbyterian church."[25] It probably didn't hurt that he preached a fiery and patriotic sermon urging men to enlist for the French and Indian War, to protect their country and their family.

When Lieutenant Colonel George Washington exhibited great bravery in that same war, Samuel made a comment about the young man that had a touch of the prophetic: "I cannot but hope Providence has hitherto preserved [him] in so signal a manner for some important service to his country."[26]

The First Great Awakening had profound social and cultural impacts on every aspect of the thirteen colonies. The ideas of equality and individual rights challenged the existing social order. The Great Awakening played a significant role in shaping the emerging American identity, fostering a sense of unity and shared purpose among the colonies, and laying the ideological groundwork for the American Revolution.

Samuel Davies went on to marry again, and undertook great effort to make sure that his children were as well-educated as he was, homeschooling them to the extent that he could around his many other duties. He was appointed the president of Princeton College when he was thirty-five but unexpectedly died two years later. But the mark he left on history was indelible. His tender heart and spirit for the Gospel, born out of the loving prayers of his parents and the suffering he underwent in his life, created a true national revival.

Years after Samuel's death, the great orator Patrick Henry would demand, "Give me liberty or give me death!" in the face of British tyranny. When he was a teenager, Henry had gone to hear Samuel Davies, and recalled him as "the greatest orator he ever heard"—no small compliment from a man who had heard the rhetoric of all the Founding Fathers.[27] Samuel's reputation continued to grow, and before the Civil War he was the most popular of American preachers, but with the burning of his church during that war, and with it, the printing press that distributed his work, his reputation dwindled into obscurity.

But some remembered. In the twentieth century, Martyn Lloyd-Jones, the renowned Welsh minister, would declare Samuel Davies the most eloquent preacher the country had ever produced.

* * *

As I have been writing about America's needing a reckoning, the more I delve into our past and the men and women who helped form the foundations we stand on, and the more I realize that what we need even more than a reckoning is an awakening. We are in desperate need of another Great Awakening! We need revival. We need the breath of the Holy Spirit to spread across our land, renewing hearts and minds. We need to repent and turn back to the principles of faith, integrity, and compassion that laid the foundations of our nation.

Samuel Davies's words "I must repeat it again, that the Holy Spirit is the only effectual reformer of the world!" ring true. This simple truth encapsulates the transformative power of the Holy Spirit. We need another Great Awakening to ignite a spiritual renewal that will inspire and guide us. I believe we are on the cusp of once again seeing a revival that will shape our nation for generations to come.

Our history is replete with movements of God that shift everything. As Samuel Davies might have observed, revival must start with a renewed heart toward worship. It has to start with thankfulness. When you look around at America today, do you see a spirit of thankfulness? Instead, we are surrounded by calls of dissatisfaction, condemnation, and ingratitude. Children's voices are amplified over those of their parents. We see people tearing down statues and disrespecting the flag.

The Catholic writer G. K. Chesterton once said, in effect, that we shouldn't tear down a fence until we know why it was put up in the first place. Everyone everywhere seems to be in a frenzy to tear down fences. But by doing this, we're cutting the ground from under our feet. How can a spirit of revival start if ingratitude and victimhood are at the center of our existence? The only way forward is one of thankfulness.

"I would maintain that thanks are the highest form of thought, and that gratitude is happiness doubled by wonder," Chesterton also said, envisioning an entire manner of life centered around thanks. "You say grace before meals. All right. But I say grace before the concert and the opera, and grace before the play and pantomime, and grace before I open a book, and grace before sketching, painting, swimming, fencing, boxing, walking, playing, dancing and grace before I dip the pen in the ink."

This is a life of revival.

Today, despite the challenges we face, we are witnessing incredible advancements in literally every aspect of life. There are almost unimaginable advancements in medicine, education, and technology. We are seeing new cures for diseases, innovative agricultural practices that increase crop yields and sustainability, and the rise of artificial intelligence that promises to solve some of our most pressing problems. These are not just achievements but opportunities for us to build a better future.

The next decade will be a time of great economic and technological prosperity. As we begin to address the broken places in our nation, Americans will come together with renewed purpose and unity. This era of prosperity and innovation will provide the foundation needed to tackle our most pressing challenges. It will pave the way for the emergence of the next generation of great Americans. This collective effort, driven by economic strength and a shared vision for a better future, could lead to transformative change and a new Great Awakening.

We need a generation of Samuel Davieses to rise up, to lead with vision and faith, and to be the answer to the challenges we face today. Together, with the guidance of the Holy Spirit, we can usher in a new era of hope and transformation. I am confident that in the months and years to come, we will once again see a revival that will shape our nation for generations. The seeds of a new Great Awakening are being planted today, and it is up to us to nurture them and battle on our knees in prayer. With the Holy Spirit's guidance, we can bring about profound and lasting change.

Lessons Learned

"WORSHIP" IS ANOTHER WORD FOR "GRATITUDE." Samuel Davies wasn't the first person to stir hearts to salvation in the Great Awakening, but he may have been the most eloquent. What makes his words so powerful, however, isn't clever vocabulary or superior wit. Many people have been brilliant without being inspiring. No, what made Samuel so persuasive was the obviousness of his sincere gratitude for God's blessings. When he spoke of Christ's love and sacrifice, his language soared with humility and wonder. He understood that revival must start with worship, and worship is just another word for gratitude.

WORSHIP GOADS US ON TOWARD TRUTH, WHICH MEANS EDUCATION. Despite Samuel's humble beginnings, his parents recognized the value of education, and this belief was central to Samuel's ministry. They understood that it wasn't enough to know a little about God—Samuel had to educate himself in the wisdom of the ages. He not only preached but also established schools to educate the next generation. This combination of faith and knowledge laid the groundwork for informed, engaged citizens, demonstrating that education coupled with spiritual guidance can lead to long-lasting societal progress. The preachers who were also teachers in these days understood that God wants us to grow, as Peter writes, "in the grace and knowledge of our Lord and Savior Jesus Christ" (2 Peter 3:18) and to follow the saying "Let the wise listen and add to their learning, and let the discerning get guidance" (Proverbs 1:5).

SPIRITUAL REVIVAL OFTEN LEADS TO SOCIAL AND POLITICAL REFORM. The Great Awakening, spearheaded by leaders like Samuel Davies, not only transformed religious life in the colonies but also fostered ideas of equality and individual rights. These principles helped shape the emerging American identity and laid the foundation for the American Revolution. Spiritual movements will always serve as catalysts for significant political and social reforms. Gratitude and knowledge can't remain bottled up. A sure sign of the spirit of revival is the desire to tell everyone the wonderful news you've heard. When that knowledge and worship transform our whole life, they spill over into every area, and that includes the political realm.

Chapter 9

DOROTHEA DIX

**Walking through Darkness,
Making Your Own Light**

Dorothea Lynde Dix was born into a world of hardship, a world that seemed to offer little hope for a young girl. She was born in Hampden, Maine, in 1802 to an impoverished and unstable family. Her father, Joseph Dix, was a wandering Methodist preacher, and her mother, Mary Bigelow Dix, was emotionally fragile and prone to long spells of depression. Their home was filled with uncertainty, and Dorothea bore the weight of responsibilities far beyond her years. When she was ten, her mother had a son, and three years later, another boy. Still young, Dorothea began to help with raising the toddler and infant.

It's a commonly accepted saying that for children raised in dysfunctional households, it can be hard to perceive God's goodness and mercy. When the only authorities in a child's life are corrupt or weak, the child often internalizes an unhealthy vision of God's character. This was true for Dorothea as well, suffering as she did from irresponsible parents. She began to develop a steely will and hard reserve, the opposite of her flighty father.

The question that Dorothea's life poses is this: How do you learn to become strong and mature when every institution in your life, from parents to society, has failed you? When you're walking in darkness, how can you make your own light?

The first failure in Dorothea's life was that of her parenting. Dorothea's father was a deeply religious man, but his intense zeal often came at the cost of his family's well-being. In those days, Maine was frontier country, and he would wander far afield to share the Gospel with those in the wilderness. He would spend hours writing religious tracts and distributing them, but while he found it invigorating to do this public work, he did little to preserve his own family. There was little money for food, and the family often went without the basic necessities of life. Meanwhile, Mary Dix was of a frail constitution, and her physical weakness morphed into mental infirmity. She couldn't care for the children, and recognizing this, she persuaded her husband to relocate the family to Massachusetts, where his relatives could help somewhat with support.[28]

It was in these moments of hunger and hardship that Dorothea's fierce sense of independence began to take shape. Even as a young girl, she felt a burning desire to break free from the cycles of poverty and instability that defined her family. She saw her father's rigid piety and her mother's emotional fragility and resolved that her own life would be different. She would not be a victim of her circumstances.

Dorothea's mother's mental illness, though not fully understood at the time, cast a dark shadow over their home. There were days when her mother barely spoke, staring vacantly out the window, disconnected from the world around her. Other days were marked by outbursts of irrational fear or sorrow, leaving Dorothea to care for her two younger brothers. Later, she would write in a letter to a friend a poignant rebuke: "You have an almost angelic mother, Anne; you cannot but be both good and happy while she hovers over you, ministering to your wants, and supplying all that the fondest affection can provide." She ended on a bitter reflection. "Your sisters, too, they comfort you. *I have none.*"[29]

As her mother's episodes became more frequent, Dorothea stepped into the role of full-time caretaker. She would prepare what little food the family had, whisper reassurances to her brothers, and try to keep the house from falling into further disarray. There were times when Dorothea would sit beside her mother, quietly holding her hand. The weight of her mother's illness was a heavy burden for a child to bear, but even then, Dorothea felt an unspoken duty to hold her fractured world together.

At the age of twelve, Dorothea made a daring decision that would alter the course of her life. Her father was in one of his spells of religious fervor and had tasked her with pasting and stitching endless pamphlets for distribution in their new neighborhood in Massachusetts. For Dorothea, tired, hungry, and overwhelmed, the boring work was the last straw.[30]

She ran away from home, determined to find a better life. She took the stagecoach to Boston, where her wealthy grandmother Dorothea Lynde Dix lived. This was not the first time she'd been to Boston. In the back of her mind, she must have stored away the happy memories of swanning around town in the chaise with her colorful and adventurous grandfather

Elijah Dix. Elijah had been born into a poor farming family, and, frustrated with the limits of their poverty, he left home at the age of twelve to board with a local minister and gain an education. He built a career as an enterprising pharmacologist, hawking elixirs to a populace that, in the days before anesthesia, was wary of surgery. Later, his investments in land would make him a wealthy man, and he augmented that wealth by taking advantage of the burgeoning Bostonian merchant fleet to import new drugs.

He also bought large tracts of land in Maine, which is where he was when he was suddenly and inexplicably murdered. But in the years before his death, Dorothea remembered being coddled by the colorful and somewhat piratical old speculator. Above all, she remembered the vast mansion he'd built on the back of his merchant wealth. It was to this mansion that she made her way at the age of twelve.[31]

When Dorothea arrived at her grandmother's house, she was barely more than a child, but her eyes held a fierce determination far beyond her years. She stood in the shadow of the imposing front door, exhausted from her journey, with only a small bag of belongings and an overwhelming sense of hope. Her grandmother was a formidable woman with little patience for nonsense, but when she opened the door and saw her granddaughter standing there, her stern expression softened—if only slightly.

"Grandmother," Dorothea began, her voice steady despite the lump in her throat, "I need to live here. I need to learn; I want to be educated!"

Her words were direct, tinged with both desperation and determination. Dorothea's grandmother studied the girl before her.

Perhaps she recognized something of her late husband's fire in this child. After a long silence, she nodded curtly. "You may stay, but you will follow my rules." It was a simple agreement, but it was all Dorothea needed. She had won her first battle, and it would not be her last. Presumably at some point, Dorothea's parents discovered her new whereabouts. They didn't seem to care.

In her grandmother's stately home, Dorothea found the stability and structure she had longed for. But "Madam Dix," as she preferred to be called, was a strict, austere woman who demanded perfection. Under her roof, young Dorothea was expected to behave like a proper lady, to learn the manners and refinement of the upper class, a world so different from the one she had known. She felt oppressed and lonely. She threw herself into her studies, fueled by a hunger for knowledge and a desire to rise above the circumstances of her birth.[32]

When a year had passed, Dorothea was sent back to Worcester, where her brothers were being raised by some of her father's relatives. She returned—older, wiser, but still bearing the same fierce sense of responsibility. She was tasked with helping raise the boys.

It was during these years that Dorothea discovered her love for teaching and education. At the age of fourteen, she began to tutor other children, and by sixteen, she had not only taken full responsibility for raising her brothers but had also opened her own school for young girls. Teaching became a calling, a way for her to influence the world around her and bring structure and purpose to the lives of others, just as education had done for her. Yet even as she built a successful life for herself, Dorothea never forgot the pain and uncertainty of her childhood, as much as she tried. She deliberately destroyed all the records of her childhood that she could. "I never knew childhood," she would later say.[33]

In teaching other children, Dorothea somewhat overcorrected by leaning too hard into her own authoritative side. She altered her clothes to make them longer and more like those of an adult. But the children under her care thought this was an unnecessary move—she was already a terror to any child who wanted to step out of line. She turned her mighty will toward giving them a good education, and this she did, with effortless and premature authority.[34]

So now all the major qualities of Dorothea's character were established. Her reserve, her inflexibility, her independence, and her bleeding heart for the suffering of the vulnerable. She was determined that others should not go through the things that she had, and she took it upon herself to be a mother for more than just her brothers.

As her grandmother aged, Dorothea took on more responsibility running the Dix mansion. By this time, she had finally found a friend to whom she could truly pour out her heart, Annie Heath. In one letter, she revealed how much the beauty of God's creation helped her cope with her frequent illnesses.

> Last night, dear Annie, I could not sleep, and after several restless hours rose at one o'clock, wrapped myself warmly in my flannel gown, and was in search of my medicine, when the remarkable clearness of the sky drew me to my window. There was Orion with his glittering sword and jeweled belt, Aldebaran, the fiery eye of Taurus, Saturn with his resplendent train of attendants... thousands on thousands of starry lamps lent their brightness to light up the vast firmament

that canopied the silent earth, — silent, for sleep had exerted its restoring influence upon all save the sick and sorrowing. I turned reluctantly again to seek my weary couch. With feelings of gratitude to my God for all his past goodness and humble trust in his future care, I laid my head on my pillow, and though I could not sleep could meditate.[35]

Throughout these years, Dorothea started seeking ways to be useful. She started another girl's school in 1831. But the strain of her relentless work schedule and buried family trauma was about to take its toll. "You are doing too much for others," a friend warned her. "You must remember you cannot do everything."

She slowly slipped into an overwhelming depression, which led to her traveling to a mental asylum in England, the York Retreat. The institution was highly unusual for the nineteenth century, eschewing the then normal practices of confinement and harsh punishment for the mentally ill. For Dorothea, who must have had significant unprocessed pain from years upon years of premature responsibility, the retreat represented a healing oasis. She stored away the lessons she learned there. Surely there was some way she could employ them back at home.[36]

And there was. Three years later, Dorothea's life took a significant turn when, while teaching a Sunday school class at the East Cambridge jail in Massachusetts, she witnessed firsthand the horrific conditions in which the mentally ill were kept. She saw men and women barely clothed, locked in cold, filthy cells, subjected to inhuman treatment. It was here, amid the stench and the suffering, that her calling crystallized.

"I must do something!" she said to the entire jail cell, with a fierce look in her eyes. "I *will* do something!" she reiterated before turning and walking out of the cell.

The next several months were some of the darkest in Dorothea's life. The wretched conditions, the cold, damp confines of the mentally ill being held in the East Cambridge jail consumed her. She couldn't dispel the stench of human suffering, the horror of these men and women abandoned by society, forgotten and treated as less than human. She had witnessed poverty, sickness, and loss before, but never had she seen such raw human misery—souls discarded, left to languish in filth, denied even the dignity of clothing.

In her darkest moments, as Dorothea prayed and dreamed about what she could do to change this, she felt the flicker of hope she'd carried for so long begin to dim. This was a level of cruelty and apathy she could scarcely comprehend. How could people—how could a society—allow such a thing to happen? She felt herself teetering on the edge of despair, questioning the goodness of God she had always believed in. Yet it was in that very moment that something shifted deep inside her. The horror of what she had seen did not break her; it galvanized her. It was as if the weight of that jail cell—the cold stones, the rusted iron bars, and the broken people behind them—became the foundation upon which her life's purpose would be built. Kneeling in prayer, Dorothea felt God's purpose for her life with clarity and resolution.

And in that moment, her course was set. Dorothea Dix, once a girl born into a dysfunctional home, became the woman who would change the way America cared for its mentally ill. This was her crucible—her dark night of the soul—and it was through this darkness that her fierce and unyielding light began to shine.

Dorothea embarked on a crusade, driven by the conviction that every life was precious and every soul deserved dignity. Her faith in God, the cornerstone of her belief, told her that Christ had come for the oppressed, the broken, and the cast-off. If that were true, then the mentally ill needed care, love, and a place where they could heal, not languish in torment. This belief was rooted in the Judeo-Christian values of compassion, mercy, and justice, which formed the bedrock of her reform efforts.

For years, Dorothea tirelessly toured the country, investigating the conditions of prisons and asylums, compiling reports and advocating for reform. Her approach was meticulous and systematic. She knew that sentiment alone would not move lawmakers; she needed to gather irrefutable evidence and present it with a moral force backed by scripture and a sense of justice.

She submitted her first report to the Massachusetts legislature in 1843. The document was blunt and damning, vividly describing the cruelty and neglect she had witnessed. The result? Massachusetts reformed its facilities for the mentally ill, building more humane hospitals. And that was just the beginning.

By the time of the buildup to the Civil War, Dorothea had become a national figure, widely consulted for expert advice on how to create humane asylums. She visited Italy, and drew the pope's attention to the poor conditions in asylums there. At her promptings, he investigated himself, and thanked her for her efforts.

Perhaps her most significant brush with history, however, was one she refused to admit in public. Living in Baltimore in 1859, she was privy to many conversations among the upper classes that persuaded her of how strong the anti-Unionist sentiments were. While Maryland didn't end up seceding, there was a very real threat that it might—a thought that plagued the new president-elect, Abraham Lincoln. On his way from his home in the north to the White House, Lincoln was to carry out a widely publicized tour from city to city. Dorothea, with her ear to the ground, found Lincoln's plans alarming.

In the years she had spent working to build hospitals, she had come to know prominent Southerners and was now familiar with their sentiments. She knew that if Lincoln came through Baltimore, there was a very real chance that a ring of secessionist thugs would carry out their plans to assassinate him. In fact, she believed worse was possible—the secessionist plots included plans to sabotage railroads and telegraph lines and ultimately seize control of the capital.

But what could she do to stop it? Surely, someone else could handle it.

No. Dorothea knew she had to do something, whatever the consequences. She was never one to shirk responsibility. So one day, she made her way to the office of Samuel M. Felton, the head of the Philadelphia, Wilmington, and Baltimore Railroad.

Felton must have been baffled when, the instant the door of his office closed behind her, Dorothea burst into an urgent narrative, rambling from assassinations to bombings to the existence of a "Southern confederacy." She talked for an hour, finally unburdening herself of this fearful responsibility, which—as she so often had—she carried alone.

At last, Dorothea stopped, watching carefully for the effect of her words.

Felton nodded. "Miss Dix, I have heard similar rumors, but only in numerous and detached parcels. Never have I heard it before related in such a tangible and reliable shape."

Persuaded by her careful and insightful intelligence-gathering, Felton sprang into action, alerting Allan Pinkerton, the detective he employed, to determine whether these assassination threats were real. They were. Word made its way to Abraham Lincoln himself, and he agreed, with some prompting, to cancel his Baltimore stop and pass through the city incognito, smuggled by Pinkerton's agents.

The secessionist plans were foiled. Lincoln arrived safely in Washington, and though his political enemies made hay of his surreptitious behavior, history should regard Dorothea's actions as having changed the outcome of history. Without her ability to step up in a crisis, the American Civil War might have turned out very differently.[37]

Dorothea went on to influence reforms across the country, bringing Christian compassion into public policy. By the time of her death in 1887, she had helped to establish more than thirty hospitals for the mentally ill, significantly shifting the cultural view of mental illness from one of criminality to one of medical need. Her faith, her belief in the sanctity of human life, and her determination to be God's hands on earth drove this transformation.

***

Dorothea grew up lacking the basic institutional support that every child should have. She lacked a father and mother who would protect and nurture her. Her grandmother gave her money but not affection. She had to step up far earlier than a child should. But her story also demonstrates that poverty and suffering should never define a person's life forever. Dorothea turned her pain into an opportunity. She became the mother that so many people, from her brothers onward, never got to have.

She could be imperious and proud, but her steely-mindedness was what made her a reformer for the ages, and ultimately gave her the courage and vision to save the life of one of the greatest American presidents.

The "dark night of the soul" is something every person will encounter at some point in their journey. The phrase was coined by Saint John of the Cross, and it refers to a period of spiritual desolation when one feels abandoned by God or lost in life's sufferings. But what Saint John—and Dorothea Dix—knew is that the dark night is not the end of faith but its most profound test, a necessary passage to spiritual maturity and a ruthless trust in God's greater plan.

Dorothea learned, as we all must, that the dark night is a refining fire. It strips us of illusions and self-reliance and draws us closer to God, forcing us to rely on Him when all other supports fail. It is necessary for true faith to grow.

I believe that the United States is in the midst of her own dark night of the soul, a period of profound trial and reckoning that weighs heavily on the collective spirit of the nation. Division, disillusionment, and discord seem to touch every corner of our society. It's as though the foundation of the country is being tested, shaken by forces that question our shared values and challenge the very idea of what it means to be American. The sense of unity that once bound us together feels frayed, and many wonder if the ideals that built this great nation can survive the storm.

But, like all dark nights, this is not the end of the story. We are not walking through this crucible to be broken; we are walking through it to be refined. This is the moment when the soul of our nation is being tested, and through the trial, we will emerge stronger, our faith deeper, our foundation firmer. Just as Dorothea Dix stood in the darkest corners of human suffering and found her calling, so too must we stand in this moment and remember who we are—a people built on faith, resilience, and the unshakable belief that with God, all things are possible.

This dark night is not about tearing us apart but about renewing our commitment to the values that truly matter. The trials we face are pushing us to reassess, to return to our foundations, and to remember that real growth comes through struggle. Just as individuals must walk through their own personal crucibles to grow stronger in faith, so too must our nation. We are not lost; we are being forged. The fires of division and hardship will temper us, refining the core of our shared beliefs in liberty, justice, and the inherent dignity of every human being. What feels like breaking is actually strengthening—what feels like the end is just the beginning of a more united, faithful, and resolute America.

Lessons Learned

BREAKING THE CYCLE IS POSSIBLE, AND IN FACT, SUFFERING OFTEN LEADS TO WISDOM. Dorothea Dix's experience in the East Cambridge jail was her personal dark night of the soul, the moment when she came face-to-face with the horrors of human suffering and the neglect of the mentally ill. It was a crucible that nearly broke her, yet it was also the moment that galvanized her. The dark night is a necessary part of life, a refining fire that burns away illusions and self-reliance, drawing us closer to God. Through these times of trial, faith is strengthened, and a deeper purpose is revealed. Just as Dorothea emerged from this darkness with a new mission, we, too, must trust that the dark nights we face can lead to growth and transformation.

COMPASSION IS A CORE VALUE! Dorothea's reform of mental healthcare was grounded in the belief that every life holds intrinsic value and every person deserves dignity and care. This fundamental Judeo-Christian principle shaped her work and legacy. Her conviction that the mentally ill should be treated with compassion and mercy was not just a moral stance but a spiritual one rooted in her understanding of Christ's teachings.

A NATION'S DARK NIGHT IS NOT THE END. The United States is going through its own dark night of the soul, but this is not a moment of defeat. Just as Dorothea's moment of despair led her to a life of purpose, our nation's trials are opportunities for refinement. This time of division and uncertainty is a crucible that can strengthen our faith, restore our foundations, and deepen our commitment to the values that truly matter—faith, justice, and dignity for all. We must trust that this dark night is not the end but a necessary passage toward a stronger, more unified future. The first step to revival is gratitude, but then knowledge: What can we learn from our own dark night?

Chapter 10

FRANCES SCOTT

The God of Miracles Acts on Faith

Mama didn't love football. She loved me, and I loved football, but there were limits to what she allowed me to do. I remember the day I told her I wanted to play. I stood at the breakfast table and told Mama that not only would I be good, I would be great. I remember standing as tall as my seven-year-old frame could manage so she would take me seriously. I had no doubt about my future.

"Timmy," Mama said, "we don't have the money for you to play football."

"Mama," I countered, "I can get most of my equipment from the school. It will barely cost anything at all!"

"Timmy." Mama placed a hand on my shoulder. "What do I do for a living?"

The seeming change of subject confused me. "You work at the hospital."

"That's right," she said matter-of-factly. "And not a week goes by where I don't see some young man come in with a football injury. Twisted ankles, concussions, knee and shoulder injuries, sprains and fractures." Mama turned all her attention to me. "All of these cost money that we don't have."

And just like that, my dream came crashing down. For the moment, at least, the conversation was over. That night, while staring at the ceiling, I came up with a plan. I was going to ask again, but this time, I would ask in a language Mama understood! The following morning, I tried again. "Mama, you always tell Ben and me to dream big. You always tell us that we can do anything with our lives. You say that nothing is impossible."

"Timmy, if you are going to quote scripture to me, at least quote it correctly," Mama chided. "Matthew 19:26 says, 'With God all things are possible.'"

"Well, I think God wants me to play football," I said. This was my bold plan. Mama loved it when we talked about God. She would drop anything she was doing to have these kinds of conversations.

"Is that right?" Mama couldn't hide the amusement in her eyes.

"Don't you and Grandmama always say that God wants me to be happy?"

"Again," Mama said with a rueful grin, "if you are going to quote scripture to me, at least have the decency to quote it correctly. Psalm 37:4 states, 'Take delight in the Lord, and He will give you the desires of your heart.'" Mama leaned in with an even bigger smile. "Or perhaps you are referring to Proverbs 16:3, which states, 'Commit to the Lord whatever you do, and He will establish your plans.'"

"Um, yes?"

"You do realize that the first part of Psalm 37 says, 'Take delight in the Lord,'" Mama said. "Have you?" She leaned back and crossed her arms over her chest. "Been taking delight in the Lord?"

"Um, yes?" I said.

Mama let out a burst of laughter. After a moment, she looked me in the eyes and said, "Timmy, I will allow you to play football on one condition."

"Thank you! Thank you! Thank you!" I stood up and wrapped my arms around her neck.

"Don't thank me yet," she said sternly. "If you get hurt, football is over. We cannot afford all the hospital bills. So the day you come home with an injury is the day you tell your coach you are done with football."

I never forgot this conversation. I loved football with all my heart. In my senior year of high school, an injury finally slowed me down. I did play my senior year and even my first year in college, but after the accident, it was never the same. But especially for those first few years of playing, I hid more injuries from Mama than I can remember: sprains, twisted ankles, and potential concussions. I remember coming home from a game with my shoulder throbbing to the point that the pain was almost all-consuming. I gritted my teeth through dinner and barely slept that night or much of the following week. For the next few days, I was worried that something truly bad had happened. Luckily, I was young, and whatever it was sorted itself out over the next couple of weeks.

I tell this story because for years, I was terrified that Mama would be true to her word and make me quit. I can't overstate just how much I loved football. It was for this reason that I didn't tell Mama when I injured my neck. I remember the exact play where the injury happened. I was scrambling in the backfield, trying to evade a tackle, when a defensive safety rushed in to bring me to the ground. Instead of leading with his shoulder or wrapping his arms around me, he lowered his head and drove the top of his helmet into the back of my neck. I went down in a heap and immediately knew something was wrong. I was also twelve and hopped up on adrenaline, so the full reality of the injury didn't register until after the game.

I remember the pinching pain and the distinct feeling that something was wrong. Later that evening, I struggled to sit down at the dinner table. I often had to move gingerly after a game, but this was different, and Mama noticed right away. In a flash, she was by my side, asking questions and gingerly prodding my neck. It didn't take long for her to also realize something was wrong.

An hour or so later, we were in the emergency room of St. Francis Hospital, where my mother worked. I remember the look on the doctor's face when he asked if he could speak to her privately. Moments later, there was a flurry of doctors laying me on my back and placing a band with thirty-pound sandbags on either side over my forehead so I couldn't move my neck even if I wanted to. I remember the nurses cutting off my shirt as they tried to speak in reassuring tones.

"Mama?" I could feel the tears running down my cheeks. "Mama, what's happening?" But at that point, Mama had been ushered out of the room so the doctors could work. I remember the feeling in the pit of my stomach as I did everything in my power not to throw up.

Over the next few hours, the doctors would show my mama and my grandmama the X-ray. My neck was broken. Hours turned into days. I spoke to Mama about it recently, and neither of us can remember exactly how many days I lay on that hospital bed. But we agreed that it was somewhere between three and seven.

During those endless days, all I could do was stare at the ceiling. Yet this time there were no flights of fancy or dreaming with God. I was terrified, wondering, *Will I ever play football again?* It was the least of my worries. *Will I ever walk again? Has the rest of my life just changed forever? How could I do this to Mama? She can't afford to take care of me!* The visions dancing through my head were dark, to say the least. I was physically ill more than once at the simple thought of the trauma that could lie ahead.

This is when the miracle happened. I've already told you about my grandmama and mama. In the introduction to this book, I painted a picture of these powerful women of God. And from the very first hour, they were praying for me. Grandmama had the entire church praying for me. I am quite certain she had the entire community praying for me, whether they believed in God or not! Grandmama believed in the God of miracles.

One night, Grandmama had a dream. She was standing in the kitchen when suddenly, a plate fell to the floor and broke in half. As she bent down to pick up the pieces, when her hands touched them, the plate was suddenly whole. Grandmama woke up with the Holy Spirit whispering to her: *Timmy is healed!*

The following morning, Grandmama marched into my hospital room and demanded that the doctors take another X-ray. The doctors disagreed. It was too soon, and the X-ray they already had was clear. "We need to wait until the swelling goes down a little more before we take another," the doctor told her.

"Timmy is healed," Grandmama said matter-of-factly. "There is nothing wrong with his neck. We need you to take another

X-ray now, please." Grandmama was not a tall woman, but at that moment, she almost seemed to tower over the doctor.

"OK," the doctor said, slightly annoyed. "Yes, ma'am."

Sure enough, when the doctor analyzed the second X-ray, it showed no problems with my neck. I remember three different doctors whispering together before they finally came and told me I could go home. "Our best guess," one of the doctors said over his glasses, "is that the swelling was so bad that it obscured the X-ray and showed a fracture where there wasn't one."

"Your best guess is wrong," Grandmama said with a laugh. "Timmy was healed by the Holy Spirit, and what you witnessed today is a modern miracle!"

Mama never mentioned the hospital bills or me quitting football. She was so relieved and so grateful for God's hand in my life that she praised God every morning, and the joy in our house was palpable. In the following days and weeks, the sun shone brighter, and the grass was all the greener. And this is the beauty of miracles. This is the beauty of a move of God. Miracles have a ripple effect. Like a large boulder crashing into a lake, every move of God, every breath of the Holy Spirit, has ramifications far beyond the immediate.

My neck being healed was obviously a huge deal for me. But it also bolstered the faith of everyone in our family, and everyone in our community. I hope this story has bolstered the faith of everyone reading these words as well. Every time I look back on those days, I can't help but spontaneously praise God. I fully believe that the God of miracles is as alive today as at any time in our history.

I don't pretend to understand why God chooses to act in some moments and not in others. Rather, let me say that differently: I believe that God is moving in all circumstances, all the time. What I don't understand is why some experience healing and others go their whole lives dealing with an injury or illness. I don't claim to understand how His goodness works. But I do know that the God of miracles is alive and well today. I know this because I have experienced Him! I know that He is moving all across the world and this land. He has been moving throughout the history of this great nation.

Not all miracles are like the ones I experienced. Most are facilitated by others. You and I have the ability to be the miracle in someone's life. When you or I choose to step out in faith or stand up to darkness, we become conduits for the Holy Spirit. Every day, all across this nation and this world, miracles are happening. We just need the eyes to see them.

I have written about the need for a reckoning. But there can be no reckoning that is not followed by a revival. A reckoning in and of itself doesn't lead anywhere. The come-to-Jesus moment our country greatly needs must be followed by a move of the Holy Spirit. A return to integrity and a return to Judeo-Christian values alone mean little if there is no room for revival. We still follow the God of miracles. The God who guided the stone from the sling of a young shepherd boy is the same God who healed my neck.

Every chapter in this book tells the story of miracles, both large and small. Every story so far has been the story of the Lord God moving through people and moments in our history. The prayers of my grandmama and my mama are still being felt today. Prayers don't have a shelf life! The God of miracles isn't confined to the pages of the Bible or to the distant past—He is the God of today, the God who listens to our prayers, and He still heals and transforms.

Our country doesn't just need men and women of integrity.

We don't just need to fight first on our knees. We don't just need a reckoning or an awakening; we need to allow the God of miracles to transform our hearts and minds. I believe a great move from God is coming. And as in the past, it will sweep our nation. But we must be ready. Pray with me for our future!

Lessons Learned

LIFE'S CHALLENGES OFTEN LEAD TO MIRACULOUS MOMENTS. My neck injury seemed like the end of the road for more than just my football dreams. Yet it was the prayers of my grandmama and mama that ushered in miraculous healing. This wasn't just a medical anomaly—it was a moment where the Holy Spirit intervened, turning what could have been a tragedy into a testimony of God's healing power. The moment served as a powerful reminder that even in our darkest hours, God can perform miracles that defy human understanding.

FAITH IS A CATALYST FOR MIRACLES. When Grandmama received the dream that I was healed, her faith was absolute. She didn't hesitate to confront the doctors and demand another X-ray, even when they were skeptical. Her steadfast belief in the God of miracles not only brought about tangible healing but also demonstrated the power of unwavering faith. This serves as a reminder that miracles often require us to step out in bold faith, trusting in God's timing and power, even when the situation seems hopeless.

THE NEED FOR A REVIVAL IN OUR NATION IS INTERTWINED WITH OUR BELIEF IN THE GOD OF MIRACLES. As I reflect on the chapters of this book, I see the Holy Spirit's hand in every story, from personal moments of healing to large-scale movements in our nation's history. We need more than a return to values; we need the God of miracles to sweep across our land, transforming hearts and minds. The prayers of my grandmama and mama, as well as the prayers of countless others, still resonate today, and I believe that God is preparing to move in miraculous ways once again. The revival we need is one that invites the miraculous power of God to heal, restore, and guide us into a brighter future. Above all, we need to recover a spirit of thankfulness. How are we to expect miracles and healing when we take for granted the blessings we already have?

Chapter 11

JIM LOVELL

"The Spirit of God Moved upon the Face of the Waters"

April 11, 1970

Jim Lovell stood in the brightly lit, cavernous room of the Kennedy Space Center. The feeling in the room was electric. Excitement, wonder, and anticipation painted every face. This was it. It was actually *it*.

The world's most-traveled man took most things in stride. Jim had been to space on three separate missions and was widely regarded as one of the most experienced astronauts alive. But this mission was different. It was going to be the first time he'd step on the moon. He couldn't believe it was finally happening.

The days of buildup had been full of emotion and anticipation. Jim's wife, Marilyn, had been encouraging and cheerful, but he knew she felt more anxious about this trip than she had about the ones before. She felt he was pushing it too far. Right now, for the cameras, she was playing the brave astronaut's wife—holding it together not only for the country but also for the Lovells' four children. Jim's heart surged with pride. He knew that, as with so much of this insane process, much of the optimism was bravado covering worry. That was the job.[38]

Jim was close friends with Neil Armstrong, Buzz Aldrin, and Michael Collins, having trained with all of them at various times. He had been happy that Buzz and Neil had been the first humans to walk on the moon nine months earlier, but he would have been lying if he had said he wasn't jealous.

It had been a profoundly spiritual moment when Jim watched his friend take that historic "one small step for man." Jim had felt the goodness of God and the grandeur of creation. The experience wasn't any less miraculous for him to watch, knowing all he did about what could go wrong; it might have even been more miraculous. The intricate dance of science, faith, and sheer willpower unfolding before his eyes was a testament to the divine and human spirit working in harmony.

If all went according to plan, this mission would result in the third time that humans walked on the moon. The mission was simple. Jim and his crew were to explore the Fra Mauro formation on the moon by deploying scientific instruments and collecting geological samples. The Fra Mauro formation was important because it was believed to be a part of the moon's Imbrium Basin, a large and ancient impact crater. Studying this area would provide critical insights into the moon's geological history and the processes that had shaped its surface. By analyzing Fra Mauro's rock and soil samples, scientists hoped to better understand the timeline of lunar impacts and volcanic activity, shedding light on the broader history of the solar system. This mission held the potential to unlock secrets about the early days of the moon and, by extension, Earth, making it a cornerstone in humanity's quest to unravel the mysteries of our celestial neighborhood.

As Jim prepared for this mission, he felt a mix of pride, nerves, and a deep sense of purpose. His mission aboard Apollo 13 was his chance to contribute to humanity's greatest adventure, to add another chapter to the story of exploration. This mission was not just another assignment; it was the culmination of years of hard work and dedication. Jim understood the significance of the journey—not only for the scientific discoveries NASA hoped to achieve but also for the inspiration it would provide to millions of people around the world. As he suited up and went through the final checks, he thought of his family, his fellow astronauts, and all those who had come before him, paving the way for this moment.

Later, Commander Jim Lovell and his men, Jack Swigert and Fred Haise, were strapped into the Saturn V rocket. This rocket, a testament to human ingenuity and determination, stood ready to propel them into history. As the countdown began, Jim remembered the sense of excitement and culmination he'd felt on his first space voyage, on Apollo 8. He'd grown up obsessed with planes and rockets, hero-worshipping Charles Lindbergh. *I'm finally doing it*, he thought. Finally, space was to become a reality and not an abstraction. His name would be added to the great list of explorers down the ages.

Now his eyes darted to the countdown timer, each number bringing the astronauts closer to the heavens. The ground trembled as the engines roared to life, and Jim felt the familiar g-forces press him into his seat. *This is why I am alive. This is what I was created to do!* The thought floated through his mind as the Saturn V rose toward the sky. The launch was flawless, and seconds later, the men hurtled through space, leaving Earth behind.

For the following two days, everything went as expected. The craft glided through the vast expanse of space, the Earth a distant blue marble behind them. On an earlier flight, when Jim had lifted his thumb and found he could completely hide the blue dot, he was struck by the humbling knowledge that he had blotted out the five billion members of humanity on the planet. "Everything I ever knew was behind my thumb. My world suddenly expanded into infinity. Out there was the Earth, 240,000 miles away." He thought about what Earth's "position was in space . . . a mere speck in the Milky Way galaxy."[39]

It reminded him of going through a tunnel while riding in the back seat of a car, and looking out the back window to see the glowing entrance shrink into the distance.[40]

How unlikely it was, he thought, that he had been born on such a planet, where all conditions were perfectly aligned to preserve and nurture life. "I arrived on a planet of the proper mass to have the gravity to sustain water and an atmosphere—the very essentials for life. I arrived on a planet just the proper distance from a star. . . . I thought to myself, I'm pretty lucky. . . . God had given mankind a stage on which to perform and how that program was going to turn out? Up to us."

We always think about death as the entrance to heaven—but what if we'd been missing the heaven all around us? He felt overwhelming gratitude and wonder wash over him.

Now he had that feeling to draw on. Communication with mission control was steady, and their voices had a reassuring connection to home. Nearly two days in, the capcom commander back on Earth summed it up: "The spacecraft is in real good shape as far as we are concerned. We're bored to tears down here."[41] That feeling wouldn't last. On April 13, fifty-five hours and fifty-five minutes into the mission, everything changed.

A loud bang reverberated through the spacecraft, followed by a jolt that shook Jim and his crew. Alarms blared, and the calm environment of the command module turned chaotic. "Houston, we've had a problem," Swigert's voice crackled over the radio, the understatement of the century.

Jim's mind raced as he scanned the control panel. Oxygen levels were dropping rapidly, and it became clear that one of the oxygen tanks had exploded. The command module, Odyssey, was critically damaged. The years of training and previous missions barely tamped down his anxiety as Jim assessed the situation. At first, the astronauts couldn't see the extent of the problem, since the instruments seemed to be going haywire. Maybe everything was fine! But as they investigated, it became horrifyingly clear that something was terribly wrong. Out the window, Jim could see white fragments of the destroyed tank floating in the vacuum. When one oxygen tank had blown up, it had damaged another, and that tank was now leaking. Two fuel cells were gone, a significant blow to the spacecraft's main power supply.

Oxygen and power were both in peril. The vacuum of space is a terrifying, hostile thing. Jim's memory of first looking at the moon up close was one of excitement. On that first trip, he and his fellow crew members had felt "like three schoolkids looking into a candy store window, watching those ancient old craters go by from—and [they] were only 60 miles above the surface." There'd been no fear or anxiety about returning. But the loneliness and emptiness were also sobering. The moon was totally dead. Nothing could survive there. As they orbited to the far side of the moon, where no man had gone before, they felt keenly aware of the loneliness of their position.

That loneliness was multiplied a millionfold by the crisis now playing itself out 200,000 miles from home. There was no time even to be disappointed about the missed trip to the moon. A lunar landing had become impossible; survival was their new objective.

Back on Earth, mission control erupted into controlled chaos. Gene Kranz, the legendary flight director, quickly marshaled his team of engineers and specialists. They were the best of the best, but the stakes had never been higher. Kranz's voice cut through the noise, his calm, resolute demeanor instilling order and purpose. "Let's work the problem," he said. "Let's solve the problem, but let's not make it any worse by guessing."

Lovell, Swigert, and Haise moved into the lunar module, Aquarius, which would now serve as a lifeboat. That was another worry. The lunar module was never intended to support three astronauts for an extended period, and certainly not for a journey back to Earth. It was meant to last forty-five hours, and now would need to stretch for ninety. It was built for two. It would need to house three. Resources were extremely limited, and the astronauts needed to conserve every bit of power, water, and oxygen.

Making do was Jim's nature. Jim's parents had separated when he was a baby, and his father had died when Jim was five. His mother had done her best to give him a normal childhood during the crushing pressures of the Great Depression, and he'd looked to Boy Scout leaders as surrogate father figures. In the depths of space, doing the math with pencil and paper and asking NASA control to check his figures, he felt that he'd ended up in the most bizarre, overwrought Boy Scout adventure in history. "Be prepared"? Who could prepare for this?[42]

Inside the cramped confines of Aquarius, the temperature

plummeted to near freezing, around 38 degrees Fahrenheit. Jim felt the cold seeping through his suit, biting into his bones. In the vacuum of space, where temperatures can drop to minus 454 degrees Fahrenheit, the module's fragile environment offered little insulation against the creeping chill. Jim Lovell and Fred Haise had specially designed lunar boots to keep their feet warm since their suits were designed for walking on the moon. Jack Swigert, however, was not originally scheduled for a moonwalk and lacked this gear. Instead, he had to improvise, layering extra clothes to stay warm. The frigid air made every breath a reminder of the astronauts' precarious situation. Jim's thoughts flickered to his wife, Marilyn, and their children, waiting anxiously for news. He knew the gravity of the situation and the slim chances of returning home. There was no time for fear—no time for prayer, even. It was time to use his God-given talents to preserve the lives He'd given them.

The engineers on the ground faced an unprecedented challenge. They had to devise a way to fit a square peg into a round hole—literally. The command module's lithium hydroxide canisters, used to scrub carbon dioxide from the air, were incompatible with the lunar module's system. The buildup of carbon dioxide (CO_2) was a lethal threat.

In an extraordinary display of ingenuity, the team at mission control devised a solution using only materials available on the spacecraft—plastic bags, cardboard, and duct tape. Jim and his crew followed the instructions to the letter, fashioning a makeshift adapter that saved their lives. "Never leave the house without duct tape," he muttered to himself—it would be his mantra if they made it out alive.

All they could think about was Earth. Jim recalled how, after the loneliness of that orbit of the moon years ago on Apollo 8, he'd been struck by seeing a patch of glowing color rise above the rim of the cold gray dead land. It was earthrise, "like a blue-and-white Christmas tree ball hanging in an absolutely black sky.... You see the Earth as it really is. A grand oasis in the vastness of space."[43] Another of the astronauts, Bill Anders, found the whole thing ironic. "We came all this way to explore the Moon, and the most important thing is that we discovered the Earth." Horrified by the blackness of the void and the tiny speck of Earth, Anders had felt his faith snap in two. How could God truly care about something so small and fragile?[44]

But on Apollo 13, all Jim could think about was getting back to that oasis. What every astronaut knows is that going to space means a journey in a tiny pocket of life in a dead vacuum. Life is always hanging by a thread. When people asked Jim if he'd taken a poison pill with him into space, he scoffed—if death was your last option, all you needed to do was open the door. All of this hung heavy in his mind as one instrument after another lit up with blaring alarms.[45]

Days blurred together as the crew navigated crisis after crisis. Sleep was fleeting, and Aquarius's cold, claustrophobic environment took its toll. Jim's muscles ached, and fatigue gnawed at his resolve. Yet every time he looked at Haise and Swigert, he saw the same determination mirrored in their eyes.

Those eyes were looking gaunter with every passing hour. In total, the men had lost almost thirty-two pounds among them. All three of them were desperately dehydrated. They needed to conserve the water supply so the water could be used to cool the ship's mechanisms, so they'd rationed water. Jim thought back over all his decisions. Was there anything else he could do? At this point, there was nothing but waiting. And praying.

Unbeknownst to him, back on Earth, his daughter Barbara

had fallen asleep clutching her Bible. At sixteen, she was the only one of the children to really understand what was happening. While all Jim could do was plan, all his family could do was pray.[46]

As Apollo 13 neared Earth, the final hurdle was reentering Earth's atmosphere. The damaged heat shield and makeshift repairs left little room for error. The astronauts secured themselves in the Odyssey. As they hit the atmosphere, flames enveloped the spacecraft, and communication with mission control was lost—a tense silence that seemed to last an eternity.

Inside the control room, all eyes were fixed on the monitors. Minutes ticked by, each one heavier than the last. Then, a crackle of static. "Houston, this is Odyssey. It's good to see you again." Cheers erupted, tears flowed, and the weight of collective relief washed over everyone.

Gene Kranz finally started breathing again. He knew that his team had to appear cool and collected, but in truth, he was anything but. Kranz, a cradle Catholic, prayed a private prayer of thanksgiving. Stress was part of the job, but the presence of God went with him everywhere.

"Whenever there is a fork in the road and a major decision, it's always part of God's plan," he thought. The trick was remembering this in space.[47]

***

I love the story of Apollo 13. This unbelievable moment in our history is often referred to as a "successful failure." The crew never made it to the moon, but in the face of insurmountable odds, they made it home. Jim Lovell's wife and four children didn't lose their father. The United States gained three new heroes.

The Apollo 13 mission is a great example of what it means to be an American. All around the world, in every country, the United States is seen not just as the land of opportunity but also as the land of ingenuity, resilience, determination, and unparalleled innovation. The three astronauts were in a damaged spacecraft over 200,000 miles from Earth, with barely enough air or power to hobble their way back. They faced life-threatening conditions, including a critically low oxygen supply, freezing temperatures, and limited water. Yet with the combined expertise of NASA scientists on the ground and an unwavering faith in God, their mission, and one another, they defied the odds.

Against all expectations, the crew of Apollo 13 managed to survive the perilous journey back to Earth. In so many ways, this mission underscores the uniqueness of the American spirit. It's a testament to the nation's ability to pull together in times of crisis, leveraging faith in God, creativity, expertise, and sheer willpower to achieve the impossible. Apollo 13 wasn't just about returning home; it was about proving that even in the direst of situations, Americans will rise to the challenge and turn a potential disaster into triumph.

This is just one of my favorite Jim Lovell stories. Two years earlier, Jim had been on another historic mission. Apollo 8 was the first manned spacecraft to leave Earth's orbit, reach the moon, orbit it, and return safely to Earth. This mission was crucial in testing the spacecraft's navigation and communication systems over long distances, ensuring that the technology and procedures were robust enough for an eventual lunar landing. And while that mission could easily warrant a chapter of its own, what I love most about it was what happened on Christmas Eve of 1968.

NASA recognized the historic significance of every word said on the broadcast of this early mission, especially since there was likely to be a huge audience of families at home for Christmas. But when Frank Borman, the mission commander, asked a NASA public relations official what to say, that official merely said it should be "something appropriate."

But how in the world could Borman find the words suitable to such a special moment? At the height of the Cold War, he felt honored that his government trusted him to choose his own words—what a contrast to the hypercontrolled cosmonauts of the Soviet Union!—but when it came down to it, everything he could think to say seemed unworthy of the occasion. He asked a friend, who in turn consulted a friend who worked in the Bureau of the Budget.

The answer finally came when that official asked his wife. A former French Resistance member and ballerina during the Second World War, Christine Laitin had the answer.

"Go back to the beginning," she said.

So that's exactly what they did. In a moment collectively experienced by virtually every American citizen, astronauts Jim Lovell, Frank Borman, and Bill Anders took turns reading the first ten verses from the Book of Genesis. This historic broadcast was heard by countless millions of people on Earth, making it one of the most-watched television broadcasts at the time.

"'In the beginning, God created the heaven and the earth. And the earth was without form and void, and darkness was upon the face of the deep. And the Spirit of God moved upon the face of the waters. And God said, Let there be light: and there was light. And God saw the light, that it was good: and

God divided the light from the darkness. And God called the light Day, and the darkness he called Night.... And God called the dry land Earth, and the gathering together of the waters called the Seas: and God saw that it was good.' And from the crew of Apollo 8, we close with good night, good luck, a Merry Christmas, and God bless all of you—all of you on the good Earth."

What a moment! The history of the United States is replete with Holy Spirit moments like this. Even the idea of going to outer space is so audacious and visionary that it remained only in the realm of imagination for centuries. While many cultures throughout history have dreamed of reaching the moon, it was the United States that turned this dream into reality. This monumental achievement could only have happened in America.

This story is by no means an isolated phenomenon but a recurring theme throughout American history. When faced with adversity, Americans have consistently pulled together to find solutions, overcome challenges, and emerge stronger. This is the story of America! Every story I have told in this book, the story I have personally lived, and the story each and every one of us finds ourselves in is the story of an overcomer. From our nation's very beginning, Americans have shown a remarkable ability to unite and confront challenges head-on. As I just laid out in the previous chapter, in the American Revolution, thirteen colonies, each with its own interests and identities, came together to fight for independence against the most formidable military power of the time. The power of collective effort and shared purpose was palpable, driving the fledgling nation toward a hard-fought victory and laying the foundation for the United States.

Why is it important to remember these stories? Because this is who we are! No matter how great the obstacle, we as a nation will overcome it. We will rise to the challenge, harness our ingenuity, and achieve the impossible. These stories remind us of our resilience, our determination, and our unyielding spirit. They also reflect the Judeo-Christian principles that have guided us throughout our history, playing a crucial role in every significant achievement. With unity, faith, and perseverance, there is no limit to what we can accomplish.

But there's one bigger lesson to take from the experience of astronauts as well. Jim Lovell's reaction to space was not to find Earth comparatively small and unimportant but rather to grow more and more appreciative of the gift we've been given to have been born at all. Jim felt revival happen in his heart as he looked at that retreating blue dot, hundreds of thousands of miles in the rearview mirror. Even in the depths of space, astronauts worshiped. Presbyterian Buzz Aldrin took communion on the moon, having received permission from his church. "At the time," he later said, "I could think of no better way to acknowledge the Apollo 11 experience than by giving thanks to God."[48]

So often, we can only perceive our lack of gratitude when the thing we have taken for granted is snatched away. We only know what we have in its absence. Very few of us will be astronauts, but hopefully, through reading their stories, we can recover our gratitude for what we take for granted, without needing to lose it. We should study the vivid photos of the cold and dead surface of the moon, and that famous photo of Earth peering from over the rim of the moon's barren surface, to remind us of what a gift our world truly is.

Not for nothing did King David feel his own insignificance when he looked on the stars. He prayed to God:

> When I look at your heavens, the work of your fingers,
> the moon and the stars, which you have set in place,
> what is man that you are mindful of him,
> and the son of man that you care for him?
> —Psalm 8:3–4, ESV

And yet his final takeaway is one of humility and hope:

> Yet you have made him a little lower than the heavenly
> beings and crowned him with glory and honor.
> —Psalm 8:5, ESV

Space is vast and magnificent, yet at the end of the day, human beings are the most important and valuable creation within it. It is knowledge of this fact that could give Jim Lovell and Buzz Aldrin the knowledge that David prophesied in another psalm:

> Where can I go from your Spirit?
> Where can I flee from your presence?
> If I go up to the heavens, you are there;
> if I make my bed in the depths, you are there.
> If I rise on the wings of the dawn,
> if I settle on the far side of the sea,
> even there your hand will guide me,
> your right hand will hold me fast.
> If I say, "Surely the darkness will hide me
> and the light become night around me,"
> even the darkness will not be dark to you;
> the night will shine like the day,
> for darkness is as light to you.
> —Psalm 139: 7–12

Lessons Learned

AMERICAN INGENUITY THRIVES IN THE FACE OF ADVERSITY. The story of Apollo 13 exemplifies the remarkable innovation and problem-solving abilities that emerged when the lives of three astronauts were on the line. Faced with life-threatening conditions 200,000 miles from Earth, the crew and NASA engineers devised ingenious solutions, turning a near-certain disaster into a "successful failure." This underscores the American spirit of overcoming adversity through creativity, collaboration, and resilience.

VICTORY IS NEVER JUST ONE PERSON'S; IT REQUIRES EVERY PERSON TO ACT. The teamwork between the astronauts and NASA engineers on Earth was a critical factor in the crew's survival. Mission control's ability to quickly problem-solve, inventing makeshift solutions like the carbon dioxide filter, illustrates the power of collective effort. Unity in times of crisis, combined with individual expertise, can lead to miraculous outcomes. But unity happens only if people grab the initiative and make courageous decisions. Autonomy and community go together.

OUR SHARED HISTORY OF OVERCOMING ADVERSITY STRENGTHENS NATIONAL IDENTITY. The Apollo missions, like many defining moments in U.S. history, illustrate the core aspects of the American character—resilience, determination, and innovation. By recalling these stories, we reaffirm that we as a nation are capable of uniting in times of challenge. They remind us that with faith, ingenuity, and perseverance, there is no obstacle too great for America to overcome.

Chapter 12

JOSHUA GLOVER

Freedom Must Be Defended

Sometime in 1810

Joshua Glover was born into slavery. The exact date is not known because who cared about the birthdate of a slave? In truth, even the year 1810 was a guess. From the very second he took his first breath, Joshua was considered the property of Benammi Garland, someone he would one day call "master." Joshua grew up in St. Louis, Missouri, and his life was marked by unimaginable suffering. Every day from sunrise to sunset was filled with the grueling work of maintaining the plantation: mending fencing, caring for livestock, and anything else that needed doing. Every day was a mirror of the one before, a relentless cycle of grueling labor. His living conditions were beyond harsh, characterized by inadequate shelter, poor nutrition, and a lack of basic human dignity.

Joshua's life was also marked by brutality. Enslaved people during this period often faced severe corporal punishment as a means of control and discipline. Beatings, whippings, and other forms of violence were common, and Joshua was no exception. The harsh treatment was a constant reminder of the oppression that defined his existence.

Every slave dreamed of freedom, but for most, that was all it was—a dream. For Joshua, the idea consumed him. Slaves didn't get much news from the outside, but in the early 1850s, it was clear the world was changing. The abolitionist movement was gaining momentum, its fervor echoing through the plantations and whispered among the slaves. The passing of the Fugitive Slave Act of 1850—a law that required the return of escaped slaves and imposed penalties on anyone aiding their flight, even in free states—had ignited fierce opposition in the North.

Meetings were held in secret, pamphlets were circulated, and fiery sermons decrying the injustice of slavery were delivered from pulpits. The Underground Railroad, a clandestine network of safe houses and brave souls, buzzed with heightened activity as more slaves sought freedom in the North and Canada.

Joshua had heard snippets of these developments in whispered conversations in the fields and hushed discussions in the slave quarters. Rumors of successful escapes and bold rescues spread like wildfire. Stories of men and women who had made it to freedom, aided by sympathetic Northerners, were told and retold, each tale kindling the flame of hope. The names of prominent abolitionists like Harriet Tubman and Frederick Douglass, who had escaped bondage and were now leading voices against slavery, reached Joshua's ears, becoming symbols of what could be.

On a stormy night in 1852, the moment had finally arrived. Heavy rain poured down as regular flashes of lightning momentarily illuminated the cramped quarters Joshua shared with six other men. He'd been planning his escape for weeks and hadn't told a soul. *It has to be tonight!* His eyes wandered to the window. He'd been waiting for the rainy season to start, and this storm was particularly fierce. *They don't get much bigger than this.* A surge of adrenaline shot through him as he slowly, carefully slipped out of his bed, making sure not to wake the others. Even with the noise of the storm, he had to keep silent, and each step was calculated to avoid the creaky floorboards. With one last glance back, he opened the door and slipped through, stepping into the cool night air. He was soaked through in a matter of seconds, but he barely noticed.

Joshua crouched low, his eyes scanning the shadows for any sign of movement. The rain was so heavy it almost completely obscured the overseers' quarters just a short distance away. Taking a deep breath to steady his nerves, Joshua crouched low as he moved swiftly but silently toward the edge of the plantation. He knew every path and hidden corner of the plantation from years of forced labor, and he used this knowledge to his advantage.

As he reached the tree line, Joshua sprinted into the dense forest, moving faster than he had ever moved in his life. Every flash of lightning momentarily illuminated the surrounding trees, casting harsh, eerie shadows. Joshua's imagination was working overtime, turning every shadow into the looming figures of his pursuers. But he couldn't stop. Not now. He pushed onward, deeper into the forest, his heart threatening to beat its way out of his chest.

For hours, Joshua navigated the dark woods, his senses heightened by adrenaline and fear. He knew that dawn would bring a search party, and he had to put as much distance between himself and the plantation as possible. He had chosen the stormy night for multiple reasons. Besides obscuring his initial escape, he hoped the driving rain would wash away any footprints or smell that the hounds might follow.

The storm abated as first light broke through the canopy. Joshua found a small, hidden hollow beneath a fallen tree. Exhausted, he crawled into the cramped space, pulling leaves and branches over himself for camouflage. He lay there trembling, his body aching from the night's exertion. The little sleep he managed to find was haunted by nightmarish visions of what would happen if he were captured.

Over the next few nights, every few hours or so, Joshua heard the distant shouts of men and the relentless barking of dogs. He couldn't be sure if they were searching for him or if these were the usual sounds of a nearby plantation. With every step, he half-ran, half-stumbled through the underbrush, driven by the sheer will to survive. His stomach groaned with hunger, and he was tired beyond words, but he ignored his discomfort. Putting distance between himself and his pursuers was his only focus.

At one point, Joshua stumbled upon a small cabin deep in the woods. Desperation and exhaustion left him with no choice but to approach. He knew the risks—if the occupants were hostile or unsympathetic, it could mean a swift end to his escape. But his hunger was gnawing, and he could barely stay on his feet. With a pounding heart, Joshua mustered the courage to knock on the door, hoping against hope that whoever answered might offer him some help.

The door creaked open slowly, and a middle-aged man peered out. Taking in Joshua's bedraggled appearance and the fear etched on his face, the man quickly gestured for Joshua to come inside. "Quickly, before anyone sees you," he whispered, scanning the woods behind Joshua. Once Joshua was inside, the man introduced himself as Samuel, a member of the local abolitionist network. Joshua collapsed, weeping in sheer relief.

But safety was still a long way off. After having slept, he began his odyssey in earnest. He would have to travel with care, often by night, from safe house to safe house, looking to cross into the North and to freedom. In this way, he traveled four hundred miles, hiking and dashing down roads and across tangled backwaters, wondering at every step whether he'd hear the shouts and bellows of pursuers, but carried ever onward by that sweet and inexorable call toward freedom. He navigated by the stars. At the tip of the Little Dipper lay the most important star of all: the North Star. In his mind, he heard that old song of the Underground Railroad:

> *When the sun comes back and the first quail calls*
> *Follow the drinking gourd*
> *For the old man is awaiting for to carry you to freedom*
> *Follow the drinking gourd*

Fatigue dogged him. He caught snatches of rest when he could, burrowed under a damp haystack or crouching under a bridge in a forest; only occasionally in the spare yet warm accommodations provided by brave abolitionists did he get a truly restful night's sleep. In the few moments of tranquility that he found, he would sometimes let his mind wander to the future.

What would it be like to live in safety, secure in the knowledge that he was free from any man's whip, the master of his own fate? The thought was almost beyond imagining.

After weeks of travel, with the help of the Underground Railroad, Joshua Glover crossed into Wisconsin, a free state known for its active abolitionist community. This made it an attractive destination for runaway slaves seeking freedom and safety. In particular, the city of Racine boasted a robust network of abolitionists dedicated to assisting escaped slaves. This community provided vital support and resources, ensuring that Joshua had a fighting chance at a new life.

For two years, Joshua lived in relative obscurity, finding work and blending into the community. Racine offered a semblance of peace and the hope of a new beginning. Over time, he developed friendships with his neighbors in the welcoming Wisconsin town. He almost let himself think he could let his guard down and speak freely of his past. However, in March 1854, disaster would strike.

Joshua's "owner," Benammi Garland, discovered his whereabouts and set out to reclaim him. Accompanied by federal marshals, Garland descended upon Joshua's modest home in Racine. The capture was brutal and swift. Joshua was beaten, shackled, and transported to the Milwaukee jail, where he would stay until Garland was ready to return home.

Thrown into the cell by grim-faced men, bloodied and filthy, Joshua felt a hard and absolute despair settle in his heart. All his efforts, all the trust he had built, all the world unfolding before him as a free man had been snatched away in an instant. Worst of all, it had all been legal. The Fugitive Slave Act had empowered the iron-gloved force of the Slave Power to reach into the supposedly safe Free States. Was anywhere safe? He knew that the rest of his life would be spent in punishment for daring to dream.

The betrayal had been personal. A Black freedman had accepted the reward to direct Garland to Joshua's door. Joshua felt his anger mix with despair. As the hours dragged on, he began to hear the sounds of a crowd gathering outside. The cacophony of voices drowned out any individual message, but Joshua could tell that the people were angry, and getting more so by the minute.

The crowd surged forward, their collective force like a tidal wave crashing against the jail's stone walls. The sounds of splintering wood and clanging metal echoed through the night, mingling with the cries of the gathered mob.

Inside the dimly lit jail, Joshua could hear the commotion growing louder. His heart pounded with fear and confused anticipation. The door to his cell was suddenly wrenched open, and there stood a man with a bushy beard, flanked by several others. "We're getting you out of here," the man said breathlessly.

Joshua retreated into the corner, lifting his fists.

"No!" the man said. "We're here to stop this. We're here to take you home."

The crowd was made up of abolitionists. News of Joshua's capture had spread like wildfire, igniting outrage among the local abolitionist community. One of the most vocal and fervent opponents of slavery in the area was Sherman Booth, a newspaper editor and fervent abolitionist. Determined to prevent Joshua's forced return to the South, Booth took to the streets, rallying the citizens of Racine with an impassioned call to action.

On March 18, 1854, an astonishing crowd of nearly five thousand people, almost all Christians driven by their faith and belief in justice, gathered outside the Milwaukee courthouse. The crowd, composed of farmers, laborers, and shopkeepers, stood shoulder to shoulder, united by their shared belief in God and human dignity. Booth had persuaded a judge in Racine to give him a warrant to arrest the slave catchers.[49] But no one there could have been under any illusions about the risks they were taking by breaking federal law. The people of Racine saw Joshua's capture as a plain case of kidnapping one of their neighbors. Together they made these resolutions, which were later printed in the paper:

> *Whereas, A colored man by the name of Joshua Glover, was kidnapped four miles from our city, last night about 8 o'clock, who was at the time of his arrest at work for one of our citizens, and was also a faithful laborer and honest man.*
>
> *Resolved, that we look upon the arrest of said Glover as an outrage upon the peaceful rights of this community, it having been made without the exhibition of any papers by first clandestinely knocking him down with a heavy club and then gagging and binding him by brute force, and carrying him off.*
>
> *Resolved, That we as citizens of Racine, demand for said Glover, a fair and impartial jury trial, in this the city where he has been arrested, and that we will attend in person and aid him by all honorable means, to secure his unconditional release, adopting as our motto the Golden Rule.*[50]

As dusk fell, Booth and a select group of abolitionists had moved to the forefront. They knew the risks; defying federal law could lead to severe consequences. But their resolve was unshakable. With the crowd's fervor at its peak, they approached the jailhouse as Booth gave a final nod, and the group sprang into action.

Quickly overwhelming the marshals, the crowd swept Joshua out into the street and onto a waiting wagon. To Joshua, overwhelmed by the sudden deliverance, the journey through the city seemed like a celebratory parade. Every man in town seemed to be there, and all around, windows were thrown open by supporters cheering them on. Men crowded around the wagon seeking to shake his hand.[51]

In the coming weeks, he would be smuggled further north and eventually put onto a ship to Canada, where he lived out the rest of his life as a free man. He married twice, the first time to a white woman. He was finally his own master.[52]

***

The successful rescue of Joshua Glover had a profound impact on the nation, galvanizing the abolitionist movement and highlighting both the cruelty of the Fugitive Slave Act and the strength of collective action. Although Sherman Booth was arrested and imprisoned for his role in Joshua's escape, he became a martyr for the cause. Despite facing significant legal challenges, Booth never regretted his decision. He spent considerable time in jail between 1854 and 1861, tirelessly fighting his conviction and advocating for the abolitionist cause, his unwavering resolve inspiring many to join the fight against slavery.

In the mid-nineteenth century, the United States was a nation grappling with its conscience, torn between the deeply entrenched institution of slavery and the growing moral outcry against it. Churches across the Northern states became epicenters of the abolitionist movement, their pulpits echoing with fiery denunciations of slavery. Preachers cited passages such as Galatians 3:28, which declares, "There is neither Jew nor Greek, neither slave nor free, nor is there male and female, for you are all one in Christ Jesus," to argue that slavery was a profound sin against God's will. These sermons not only stirred the hearts of their congregants but also galvanized them into action, inspiring them to join the cause of abolition.

It was not just the prominent leaders and preachers who drove the movement; it was also the countless ordinary men and women who heeded the call. Farmers, blacksmiths, shopkeepers, and housewives all played crucial roles in the Underground Railroad, risking their lives and livelihoods to help escaped slaves find freedom. These everyday heroes, guided by their faith, provided safe houses, food, and guidance, creating a clandestine network that stretched across the Northern states.

In small towns and rural areas, local churches organized abolitionist meetings and rallies where congregants could learn about the evils of slavery and discuss ways to support the cause. These gatherings fostered a sense of community and shared purpose, strengthening the resolve of those committed to ending slavery. Hymns and spirituals, rich with themes of liberation and divine justice, became anthems of the movement, their powerful messages resonating deeply with those who sang them.

People love to argue about the founders and demonize the generations of men and women who came before us. It has become totally acceptable to vilify entire generations. But Joshua

Glover's story is not his alone. It is the story of thousands of men and women who put their lives on the line to free him.

The Holy Spirit moved in the hearts of men and women to shift the history of our nation as they fought for justice. The abolitionist movement was not just a political endeavor but a deeply spiritual one, rooted in the adherents' belief that they were doing God's work. Men and women felt called to act, believing they were instruments of God's will, fighting to dispel the great darkness that enveloped the nation.

The same is true today. The Holy Spirit is moving in our land. Men and women across the United States are shaping our future. In the days of Joshua Glover, it was the farmers, laborers, and shopkeepers who changed the face of our nation. The same is true today. All it takes to be extraordinary, to shift the face of a nation, is for a citizen to be willing to be the answer. The tide shifted when enough people stood up and said, "Enough!"

Darkness only makes the light shine brighter. On this side of eternity, there will always be injustice. And it is good to point it out and clearly define it. It is good to understand the problem. But understanding something is a far cry from changing it. The answer to the problem is a groundswell of men and women of faith pushing back against the darkness. The answer starts and ends in prayer. The answer to injustice is you and me making a choice to stand up for truth and righteousness. And I see it happening!

People across our nation are awakening to God's call. You can feel it in the air. The Holy Spirit is whispering to hearts and preparing the way for the next Great Awakening. Be inspired, my friends! And join me in prayer and expectation for God's next great move.

Lessons Learned

Joshua Glover's story embodies the indomitable truth that freedom cannot be suppressed forever. Born into the brutal conditions of slavery, Joshua lived a life marked by relentless oppression and inhumane treatment. His journey from slave to fugitive was driven by an unquenchable desire for freedom, a dream that consumed him. His escape on a stormy night, navigating treacherous terrain and the threat of capture, illustrates the extraordinary lengths slaves were willing to go to in their quest for liberation.

The abolitionist movement was deeply rooted in spirituality and moral conviction. Far more than a political movement, it was a spiritual awakening for many, rooted in the belief that ending slavery was God's work. Churches in the North became rallying points for abolition, with preachers inspiring their congregants to take action against the darkness of slavery. This movement wasn't led just by prominent figures but also by ordinary men and women of faith who, compelled by their beliefs, helped run the Underground Railroad and stood in solidarity with the oppressed.

The story of Joshua Glover serves as a reminder that America's heroes are as real and common as her villains. It wasn't just the famous abolitionists but also farmers, laborers, and shopkeepers—everyday citizens—who shifted the course of history. These individuals risked their lives and livelihoods to create the groundswell that ultimately brought about significant social change. Their courage reminds us that change often begins with ordinary people who choose to stand for truth and justice.

Joshua faced the reality that there were wicked people in this country, enslavers who would travel hundreds of miles to kidnap a free man or a dishonorable friend who would betray his trust. But his deliverance also demonstrates that there were true Americans who believed in community, freedom, and faith—they wouldn't let a wicked law be carried out, and their efforts were instrumental in changing it.

Chapter 13

EDDIE RICKENBACKER

Every Blessing Is Meant to Be Passed On

From a young age, Eddie Rickenbacker had a fascination with anything mechanical. He loved tinkering with machines, clocks, and any mechanical device he could get his hands on. Though his formal education was cut short after his father's death when Eddie was twelve, his curious mind was always in overdrive. He took odd jobs to help support his family, but what truly captivated him was the burgeoning world of automobiles. Eddie became known for his knack with engines, fixing cars, and racing them with reckless abandon. It was in this fast-paced world that Eddie first gained his reputation as a daredevil. His boldness on the racetrack earned him attention, eventually leading him to become a professional race car driver in the early 1910s. Speed and danger had become his closest companions.

Despite his racing success, the skies beckoned. Eddie had an insatiable hunger for adventure, and the dawn of aviation presented an irresistible challenge. He grew up not far from the Wright brothers, who achieved their historic first flight in 1903, and became friendly with Orville Wright. It wasn't long before Eddie left racing in favor of flying. These were the earliest days of human flight, and Eddie was arguably the most daring pilot to take to the skies.

When World War I erupted, Eddie found himself in the cockpit of a fighter plane. He was part of one of the first fighter plane units ever. He served in the 94th Aero Squadron, also known as the "Hat in the Ring Squadron." The unit's formation was part of the larger effort by Allied forces to develop organized and effective fighter squadrons as air combat became a critical part of warfare.

As dawn broke over the French countryside on October 29, 1918, a thick blanket of fog still clung to the ground, and somewhere in the skies above, Captain Eddie Rickenbacker sat in the cockpit of his Nieuport 28 fighter plane, scanning the horizon with a sharp, practiced eye. The steady hum of the engine was his constant companion, and the cool wind whipped against his face as he soared high above the trenches, alone on patrol.

By this point in the war, Eddie was no stranger to peril. He had already earned his place as one of the most feared and respected pilots in the skies, having shot down over two dozen enemy planes. His squadron called him "the Ace of Aces," a title earned through raw talent, unshakable courage, and a keen ability to outthink his opponents in dogfights.

Far below, the front lines of the war stretched out in a jagged scar across the landscape. The muddy trenches snaked their way across the earth, filled with soldiers huddled in the muck and mire, their faces grim as they waited for the next order, the next attack, the next moment of chaos.

Suddenly, just beyond the horizon, Eddie spotted a flicker of movement—several German Fokker D.VII fighters cutting through the clouds. He counted seven of them. They were fast, agile, and armed with the most sophisticated weaponry the Germans had developed. And they were headed directly for an American observation plane below—a slow, vulnerable craft tasked with gathering crucial intelligence from behind enemy lines.

Eddie's heart pounded. He had no backup. He was alone and outnumbered. But turning back was not an option. The men in that observation plane were sitting ducks; without his intervention, they wouldn't stand a chance. Gritting his teeth, Eddie made his decision in an instant. He banked hard to the right, pushing his Nieuport into a steep dive, racing toward the German squadron with the reckless abandon that had made him a living legend.

As he closed in, the world around him seemed to slow. Time and again, Eddie had faced moments like this—moments when everything hinged on split-second decisions and the precision of his flying. But this time, he knew, it was different. The odds were staggering—seven against one. But Eddie didn't flinch. Instead, he felt a calm determination settle over him, a clarity of purpose that came not from arrogance but from faith. He believed he was meant to survive, meant to fight, meant to win.

He pulled his plane into the center of the enemy formation and opened fire with the twin Vickers machine guns mounted on the nose of his aircraft. The staccato burst of gunfire ripped through the air, and in an instant, the Germans broke formation, scattering like startled birds. Eddie stayed on them, diving and twisting through the air, his plane moving as though it were an extension of his body.

Within seconds, he had his first target in his sights. A German Fokker banked sharply, trying to evade him, but Eddie was faster. He squeezed the trigger, and a burst of bullets tore through the enemy's fuselage. The Fokker lurched in the air before spiraling downward in flames, crashing into the earth below.

One down. Six to go.

Without missing a beat, Eddie turned his attention to the next plane. By this point in the war, the German army knew and feared Eddie's plane; it featured the "Hat in the Ring" insignia of the 94th Aero Squadron, which was easily recognizable from the air. This symbol was a red, white, and blue circle with a top hat inside it, representing the squadron's connection to Uncle Sam and American patriotism. Realizing that they were up against the infamous Ace of Aces, the Germans fought back with everything they had. But Eddie's skill and tenacity were unmatched. He dodged their fire, weaving through the sky in a deadly dance, always one step ahead of his enemies.

The second plane fell soon after the first. Then the third. Eddie was relentless, his mind focused solely on the task at hand, and his every movement precise and calculated. He knew that hesitation would mean death, and so he pressed on, flying faster, harder, pushing his Nieuport to its limits.

It wasn't long before the remaining German planes, now whittled down to just four, accepted that they were no match for the Ace of Aces. They turned tail and fled, disappearing into the clouds, leaving Eddie alone in the sky. Below him, the American observation plane continued its mission, untouched, thanks to the daring actions of the lone pilot who had risked everything to protect them.

Eddie's faith was everything to him. Before every mission, he said a prayer. Once, he recalled, God had saved him after he was attacked in France during World War I by three German Albatross planes.

> *I came out of a dive so quickly that the terrific pressure collapsed my right-hand upper wing. No matter what I tried, I couldn't come out of that whirl of death.*
>
> *I often wish I could think as fast under normal conditions as I did during that drop. While I fought the controls and tried to get the engine going, I prayed: "Oh, God," I said, "help me get out of this."*
>
> *As a last desperate act, I threw my weight to the left-hand side over the cockpit and jammed the controls, then jammed the engine wide open. The thing suddenly sputtered and vibrated violently, and the plane sailed away, on her one good wing, for France. I held it like that all the way home. . . .*
>
> *I realized then, as I headed for France on one wing, that there had to be Something else.*[53]

He prayed for others, too. "I'd ask for the strength and courage to do my duty and protect my fellow pilots. I knew that at any moment, it could be my last flight, and I trusted God to see me through. . . . There were moments in the air when I didn't know if I'd make it back, and that's when I'd pray the hardest. I believed that God had a plan for me, whatever it might be."

If Eddie Rickenbacker's story ended here, he would still be heralded as an American hero. Yet this isn't even the craziest experience he would face. Having survived World War I, he would face a test of his courage, faith, and leadership again in 1942. In what was meant to be a simple flight across the Pacific, Eddie had been sent on a top secret mission to deliver a critical message from Secretary of War Henry Stimson to General Douglas MacArthur in the Pacific Theater during World War II. Though the exact contents of the message remain unclear to this day, it is believed to have been of great strategic importance for the war effort. It was so sensitive that Eddie had to memorize it instead of committing it to paper.[54]

The fifty-two-year-old former ace pilot was now an airline executive. Despite his civilian status, Eddie's expertise and reputation made him the ideal person to carry out this mission. He was flown out to the Pacific as an advisor, and not the pilot or copilot, but the routine transport flight would soon become anything but ordinary.

About an hour before their scheduled landing on an island, the pilot descended through the clouds to a thousand feet. Somewhat awestruck by his famous passenger, he offered to let Eddie fly for about an hour, which the older man did, before the pilot took back the controls. The Pacific Ocean spread out below them like the hard blue-green shell, its edges blending into the soft colors of the growing morning.

As the minutes wore on, Eddie could see the concern in the pilot's eyes. "What's the problem?" he asked. The pilot hesitated, glancing at the instruments. "We should have seen the island by now. We should have seen it forty minutes ago."

Eddie felt his stomach drop in dread. He scanned the horizon, but there was nothing—just an endless ocean. "How much fuel do we have?" he asked. The answer came back grimly: not enough. A heavy silence settled over the cabin. Eddie knew then that the eight men on board were in serious trouble. The B-17, designed for resilience, had become a speck of metal in an unforgiving sea of blue.

Slowly, the men began to piece together what had happened.

They'd trusted the weather report they'd been given and assumed they were facing ten-mile-per-hour wind when, in fact, it must have been much greater. But even taking this into account, their instruments were giving baffling readings. Perhaps the octant had been damaged as well. They'd been in a different B-17 the day before, but the takeoff had been scratched after the plane was found to be faulty. It's likely someone had brought the octant from the other B-17 without realizing it had been damaged during that incident.

This was turning into a perfect storm, and time was running out.

Eddie had been lost in the air before but never this badly, and never with nothing below him but inhospitable saltwater. He clutched at the cane he'd used since he'd been injured in a plane crash the year before. What were the odds he'd make it out alive of a second crash? Would God spare him from death yet again?

"One hour of fuel remaining," the pilot radioed. An American operator received the message, but there was no response. It would be the last message from the crew.

Recognizing that a crash landing was inevitable, the crew began tossing things out of the plane, making split-second decisions about what to keep. Eddie instinctively wrapped a rope around himself and patted his pocket, feeling the crucifix he kept there. "Should we drink all the water?" one man asked.

"No," Eddie said. "We'll need that later."

Suddenly, the drone of the engines changed, sputtering ominously. One by one, they began to fail. The plane lost altitude rapidly as the crew scrambled in desperation. The once-mighty aircraft now lurched toward the ocean, plunging in a slow, helpless descent. The pilot brought the plane down to parallel the heavy swell of the waves, seeking to land in the trough to reduce the possibility of the plane being torn apart.

With the engines dead, there was a period of eerie silence except for the frantic sound of the radio operator still sending out useless SOS messages. In those final moments, the men braced themselves and strapped themselves into their seats, hearts pounding as the ocean rushed up to meet them. And then—a deafening crash. The plane hit the water with brutal force, the impact sending shock waves through the men's bodies as equipment came loose and sharp pieces of metal shot around the plane. The radio operator was thrown into the panel, gashing his nose. Green water flooded in from a broken window. After a second crash, the plane came to a quick halt. The pilot had angled it perfectly. The plane remained afloat.

For a moment, the world was nothing but chaos. The cold, dark water surged into the cabin, and the plane groaned like a wounded beast, sinking fast. Eddie's body ached from the impact, but his mind snapped into sharp focus. "Get the life rafts!" he shouted, his voice cutting through the rising panic. One of the crew fumbled with the release mechanism, hands shaking, eyes wide with fear. The seawater mixed with the blood of the injured men as they disentangled themselves from equipment and seat belts.

They grabbed the three life rafts, hauled them toward a hatch, and clambered onto the floating wing. Eddie had to lean heavily on his cane. He and the crew had to act quickly once they were out. The sea was choppy, with swells rising to twelve feet and rocking the slippery surface of the plane's wing. The life rafts were packed with a small CO_2 canister designed to inflate them in emergencies. Eddie pulled the cord that activated the release valve on the canister. The other men did the same with their raft. The life rafts hissed loudly as the CO_2 filled their chambers, causing them to rapidly expand and take shape. Within moments, the rafts were fully inflated, bobbing just above the water's surface as the men scrambled aboard, gasping for breath.

Finally, aboard the rafts, they drifted away from the plane. Only then did they realize that they had no water. In the confusion, they'd left the water and rations on the plane, which was now slipping into the sea. "That was the worst advice you ever gave," one of the men told Eddie, who couldn't help but agree. His other choices panned out better—he used his battered old fedora to bail water in the high sea, and the men used the rope he'd wrapped around himself to lash the three rafts together. Finally, Eddie tossed his cane into the ocean with a wry smile.

"The good Lord forgot to teach me how to walk on water with it," he quipped.

Drenched and exhausted, Eddie scanned the horizon for any sign of wreckage—or, worse, enemy planes. The men looked at each other. "We're alive," Eddie muttered, more to himself than anyone else. "Now we stay that way."

The fight would be mental as much as physical. That first night on the water, Eddie felt his muscles stiffen agonizingly, with old wounds flaring up in the cold, cramped, rocking raft. He was colder than he'd ever been. But he resolved to himself that none of the other men would hear a complaint from him. For one thing, two other men were injured more seriously, but more important, someone needed to be a rock, and Eddie was much older and wiser, and a veteran of facing death. This wasn't his first rodeo.

If God had spared him all these years, it must be for this. "Somebody was going to have to hold them together," he later recalled, "and that somebody would have to be me."[55]

Even in the chaos, Eddie's leadership was clear. He rallied the men, organizing them, rationing supplies, and offering a fierce determination that kept their hopes afloat in the desolate vastness of the ocean. He warned the men not to drink seawater, as much as they might be tempted. The salt would make them thirstier than they had been before, since human kidneys aren't designed to filter out that much salt from liquid. When sharks bumped the bottom of the rafts in the middle of the night, Eddie kept his cool. One of the men asked what the sharks were doing, and Eddie brushed it off. "Well, they are just scratching their backs." Privately, he prayed that none of the animals had skin rough enough to puncture the plastic. *Thank the Lord they're not swordfish.*[56]

They had some oranges that one man had tucked into his clothes, but these ran out after three days. Knowing they had no more food to look forward to, the men spiraled into fantasizing about their favorite meals. Some of the men felt hopeful because surely the American government must be using every tactic it could to search for the famous Captain Rickenbacker, Ace of Aces. With each passing day, that hope dwindled.

Eddie realized they needed their thoughts pushed in a more positive direction. Each day, sometimes twice a day, he led the men in prayer. He encouraged them to hold on, reminding them that God had not abandoned them, even in the face of such overwhelming odds. "I have found that prayer works when all else fails," he later said of the ordeal.

One man had a little New Testament. He would read a passage and pass the book to the next man. For some, it was their first experience with scripture. Eddie found "new beauty" in the familiar, comforting phrases of Psalm 23, and a fresh appreciation for a less-known passage in Matthew 6:31–34 (KJV):

Therefore take no thought, saying, What shall we eat? or, What shall we drink? or, Wherewithal shall we be clothed? ... For your heavenly Father knoweth that ye have need of all these things. But seek ye first the kingdom of God, and his righteousness; and all these things shall be added unto you. Take therefore no thought for the morrow: for the morrow shall take thought for the things of itself. Sufficient unto the day is the evil thereof.

They all found themselves contemplating great matters. Some of them had never considered the state of their soul, or what it might be like to meet their maker. The little society on the rafts seesawed between lamenting the everyday annoyances of a painful, long trip—everyone was in pain and short-tempered—and engaging in deep, heartfelt conversations, making long confessions of regret and loss and joy. As the days stretched on, each man came to know the others' darkest secrets. "I came to know those men—indeed we all came to know one another—better than they knew themselves," Eddie wrote.[57]

Before this, he had always kept his faith as a private thing, the angel on his shoulder as he faced death day after day in the skies of France. On the water, all embarrassment went away. He spoke openly and candidly about his devotion, and felt God's certainty grow in his heart.

And then, just as things seemed their darkest, something miraculous happened—a bird landed on Eddie's misshapen old hat. Eddie's breath caught in his throat. The men were starving, and this was a miracle! He felt their eyes on him, their jaws hanging open in suspense. Slowly, inchingly, he lifted his hand and suddenly clamped down, catching the bird by its legs.

Eddie killed the bird, and the men used its meat for food,

which provided them with much-needed protein. Additionally, they used the intestines as bait to catch fish, which sustained them further. The bird became a symbol of hope that God was watching over them. Even the men who were unbelievers felt heartened, and it was lost on no one that the bird had appeared right after the conclusion of that day's prayer service.

Another day, they paddled their way into a storm and caught rainwater in some buckets and the pockets of their life jackets.

But things couldn't always go well. As the days dragged on, one of the men grew worse and worse. Eddie put it together: The man had deliriously been drinking seawater at night. It was dehydrating his body, shutting it down. On the thirteenth day, they discovered him dead. Eddie laid next to him, cradling his body, hoping that perhaps they'd been wrong, that he was just cold. No. The next morning, they sadly performed a funeral at sea.

Eddie's methods of leadership weren't always so tender. He had to berate some of the men, shouting and raging to snap them out of self-pity, and some of them resolved to survive just to have their revenge on him. He found grim satisfaction in the result, for all he needed was that they desire to live, not that they like him!

Finally, after more than three weeks at sea, a plane spotted the crew. After a long moment of suspense, the plane returned and landed. It was an American navy plane, not a Japanese plane. It was there to rescue them.

The men were gaunt, sunburned, and dehydrated but alive. Eddie's leadership and unwavering faith had kept them going. As Eddie, exhausted and weak, was tied onto a wing of the plane—there wasn't enough room inside for everyone, and the sickest were prioritized—he found that all he could say was

"Thank God" and "God bless the Navy" over and over. The rescuers gave him beef broth and water. A feast!

When the plane landed and the survivors were carried to the hospital, Eddie was overwhelmed by the beauty of the nighttime island. "The route lay under beautiful palm trees through which the moon was shining. The night air was warm. What a lovely evening!"[58]

Eddie's belief that the Holy Spirit was guiding him in every situation, no matter how dire, is what sustained him. He would often speak of this later in life, reflecting on how the right person, filled with faith and guided by the Holy Spirit, can step into even the most impossible situations and become the miracle that changes everything. Whether in the skies of Europe during World War I or the vast expanse of the Pacific during World War II, Eddie Rickenbacker proved the power of faith and the belief that anyone, with God's guidance, can make a profound difference.

* * *

In his brilliant autobiography, *Rickenbacker*, Eddie wrote, "I believe that every prayer is answered in one way or another. Sometimes the answer is 'no,' and sometimes it is 'yes,' but always it is answered." Eddie was a man who fought first on his knees, but not only on his knees! He believed in the power of prayer and the power of the Holy Spirit. He was guided by his faith. But Eddie also understood that prayer and belief will only take us so far! Eddie Rickenbacker was a man of action. If something needed doing, he did it. No matter the odds, no matter the circumstances, he put his faith into action.

Eddie was not concerned about whether God's answer was yes or no. In his autobiography, he wrote, "I have found that prayer works when all else fails. The thought of death was never so near to me as on that raft, but I did not lose hope because I knew that God was with us and would see us through if it was His will."

I love those last five words: "if it was His will." This is the essence of faith! We are meant to step out in faith no matter the circumstances, and it is not our concern whether things work out. Our job is to be God's hands and feet in this world. Eddie Rickenbacker was just one man. He died in 1973 at the age of eighty-two. But the world was different because Eddie put his faith into action.

None of us knows how long we will be here or what challenges we will face. What we do know is that our time on this earth is an opportunity—an opportunity to live with purpose, to trust in something greater than ourselves, and to step out in faith even when the path is unclear. Eddie Rickenbacker understood this deeply. He didn't wait for certainty; he acted with courage, guided by his belief that God's will mattered, not the outcome.

As we look around at the challenges facing our nation today, it's easy to become disheartened. We see division, anger, and uncertainty. But like Eddie Rickenbacker adrift in the Pacific, we must hold fast to our faith. We must believe, as he did, that God has a plan for our lives and our nation. His plan is not a mystery. God's plan is you and me. God's plan is a nation of Eddie Rickenbackers rising up and stepping out in faith.

Lessons Learned

GOD BLESSES US SO WE CAN BLESS OTHERS. Eddie Rickenbacker's leadership shone brightest in moments of crisis. He didn't just survive those twenty-four days at sea—he led others through them. His concern was always for his fellow crewmen, making sure they stayed focused, rationed supplies, and held on to hope. Leadership, he shows us, is about putting the well-being of others first, especially in times of desperation.

Throughout his life, Eddie often said that it was God's will, not his own, that determined the outcome. Whether in the heat of battle or stranded at sea, he didn't concern himself with how things would end. He simply did what was in front of him, trusting that God's plan would unfold as it should. From the Bible we know that God blesses us so we can bless others. In Genesis 12:2-3, God makes clear that He has chosen Abraham not because He expects Abraham to ignore the rest of the world but so that he can in turn share his blessings. God says, "I will make your name great, and you will be a blessing. . . . And all peoples on earth will be blessed through you."

PRAYER IS POWER, BUT ACTION IS REQUIRED. Eddie believed in the power of prayer, but he also knew that prayer alone wasn't enough. He prayed for guidance and then took action. Whether leading his crew through the survival ordeal or fighting enemies in the sky, Eddie always paired his faith with decisive, courageous steps. We are reminded that faith without action is incomplete; prayer must be the catalyst for doing what needs to be done.

From the skies over Europe to the middle of the Pacific, Eddie Rickenbacker's story is full of miraculous moments. Yet these miracles often came because of his faith and willingness to act. The seagull landing on his head during the life raft ordeal was a blessing, but it was Eddie's quick reflexes and resourcefulness that turned it into food. His story reminds us that miracles often happen when ordinary people step forward with faith and courage, ready to be God's hands and feet in the world.

FAITH TRANSFORMS FEAR INTO ACTION! Eddie Rickenbacker's unshakable faith was the foundation of his courage. In moments when fear could have paralyzed him—whether facing enemy planes or being adrift in the Pacific—his trust in God allowed him to act decisively. His life teaches us that faith isn't passive; it's the force that turns fear into bold, necessary action.

Faith also empowers us to share the Gospel. Eddie said later that the biggest change he experienced after his time at sea was how his faith transformed from a private comfort to a public message. One columnist noticed it: "There is an unworldly gleam in his eyes and a quaver in his voice these days," he wrote. "Rickenbacker has become an evangelist without knowing it." Eddie included the quote in his book, but corrected him: "*I knew.* From the time of the Pacific ordeal, my faith in God was an active, open part of my life."[59]

Part III

Stewardship

Whatever you do, work at it with all your heart, as working for the Lord, not for human masters, since you know that you will receive an inheritance from the Lord as a reward. It is the Lord Christ you are serving.

—COLOSSIANS 3:23–24

Chapter 14

NORMAN BORLAUG

All Work Is Stewardship for God

Born into a close-knit Norwegian American family in 1914, Norman Borlaug grew up on a farm in Cresco, Iowa. He was the firstborn of four children, and his parents, Henry and Clara Borlaug, were devout Lutherans. Sundays were sacred, strictly reserved for church services, prayer, and reflection. The Christian faith permeated every aspect of their lives. Norman's upbringing was rooted in the belief that faith was not separate from the material world but rather provided the foundation for everything—especially farming.

To the Borlaugs, farming was more than a means of survival; it was a calling and a divine responsibility. Norman's family took great pride in their work, viewing the land as a gift from God that must be nurtured and cared for. In the part of Iowa known as "Little Norway," all the older people spoke with thick accents, and conversation floated easily between English and

Norwegian. Norman's family called him "Norm boy." The family only moved into their own home when he was eight, and though it was not insulated or electrified, it was theirs. He and his three younger sisters could sit outside on cold winter nights, huddled in blankets, and hear the Milwaukee train pulling into Cresco, echoing across thirteen still, empty miles.

"It was the one time we sensed we were part of a wider sphere," he remembered. "Those sound waves were our sole connection to the world."[60]

The wide-open spaces gave the Borlaug family a deep connection to the land. Often, while out tilling the ground or repairing fences, Norman's grandfather Nels would pause and quote scripture to Norman. One of his favorites was Genesis 2:15 (ESV): "The Lord God took the man and put him in the garden of Eden to work it and keep it." After reciting the verse, Nels would turn to Norman and say, "You see, Norm boy, we're not just farming for ourselves. This is God's land, and we are its caretakers. To care for this soil is to honor the work He set for us long ago."

As they worked the fields together, Henry would explain to Norman that their labor wasn't merely about producing crops—it was a moral duty tied to stewardship. He taught Norman that the cycles of planting and harvesting mirrored the cycles of life and faith. Each season brought its own challenges, but through perseverance and trust in God's plan, they could face any obstacle. In their household, faith and farming were inseparable, and every row they plowed was seen as part of a larger mission to serve both family and community through God's provision. However, in the world of subsistence farming, work and misery went hand in hand. Harvesting maize was a "two-month horror." As Norman picked and shucked the sharp leaves, his hands ended up chapped and bleeding despite his wearing gloves.[61]

When Norman turned fifteen, the world shifted. These were the early days of the Great Depression when all the banks and financial markets crashed, and inflation soared. Aside from the economic instability, there were also widespread crop failures and droughts across the Midwest. These years were deeply trying for farming families like the Borlaugs, as they experienced the full brunt of the economic collapse and the Dust Bowl conditions that decimated crops.

Even so, Norman's grandfather never wavered in his belief. The land gives, and the land takes away, he thought. But God is constant. We honor Him by doing the best we can with what we've been given, no matter the outcome.

He pushed his young grandson to pursue an education. It was a chance for a different life. Norm acquiesced, but without much enthusiasm. He knew he'd become a farmer like his father. What other life was possible?

In one particularly difficult year on the Borlaug farm, the weather had been unforgiving—late frosts followed by a period of drought that left the crops struggling to grow. The family had worked hard, but as the season wore on, it became clear that the yield would be far less than expected. The worry of how they would get by through the winter weighed heavily on Norman's father.

One day, after weeks of backbreaking work with little reward, Norman returned from the fields looking frustrated and angry. The boy had been doing all he could to help his father, but the results were so meager compared to the effort they were putting in. It was in that moment that Norman's father decided it was time for a deeper conversation, one that would shape Norman's outlook on everything about his life.

That evening, as the sun set over the Borlaug farm, Norman's father sat beside him, still covered in dirt and grime from the day's work. "Norm boy," his father began, "there's something I want to talk to you about, something my father told me when I was about your age."

Norman turned all his attention to his father. He could tell by his tone that whatever came next was going to be important.

"Farming isn't just about making a living—it's about fulfilling a calling."

Although Norman appreciated the truth of his father's words with his mind, his heart or perhaps his painful, hardened hands were unpersuaded.

Norman's father smiled, as if reading his mind.

"I have watched you grow up on this farm. And I have no doubt that you could be a great farmer if it's what you want. But I also have witnessed that keen mind of yours that you clearly get from your mother. Whatever you do with your life," his father said, "whether you stay here on the farm or go somewhere far away and put that keen mind to work, never forget that the work we do is meant to honor God and serve others."[62]

As he lay in bed that night, Norman stared at the ceiling and began to dream with God. He dreamed of all the possibilities far beyond the farm. Until that moment, he had always seen himself following in his father's footsteps. But now the entire world seemed to be open to him! Though it was far from easy, Norman's dreaming and determination to better himself, along with scholarships and money earned by doing odd jobs, eventually led him to enroll at the University of Minnesota.

The main thing that enabled his education, though, was the tractor that his father bought. This technological innovation allowed Henry to quadruple his harvest and invest in his children's education.

When Norman Borlaug arrived at the university, he felt as though his world had expanded in ways he could never have imagined. The boy who had once spent his days tending fields and feeding livestock now found himself in classrooms and laboratories, surrounded by people from every walk of life. But in many ways, Norman never truly left the farm. The values and lessons instilled by his father—faith, stewardship, perseverance—were woven into every step of his journey.

Norman's academic life was rigorous and, at times, overwhelming. The complexities of plant biology and genetics challenged him in ways the farm never had, but he saw them as extensions of the same calling. Now, instead of plowing fields, Norman was plowing through textbooks and experiments, yet the mission was the same: to serve others through his work.

He began to realize that the farm was not merely a place; it was a concept, a foundation for his life. The cycles of planting and harvesting mirrored the cycles of his academic journey. Just as he had faced droughts and poor yields on the farm, Norman faced setbacks in the lab. Experiments failed. Research hit dead ends. But just as his father had taught him to trust the seasons, Norman trusted the process. He saw each failure as a lesson, each challenge as a necessary part of the work God had called him to do.

During these years, Norman's faith only deepened. He spent many late nights reflecting on the connection between science and spirituality. To him, there was no conflict between the two; both were expressions of God's design. As he studied the intricacies of genetics, he often marveled at the complexity of creation. He saw his research as a way to unlock the potential God had embedded in the natural world—a way to make the land more fruitful, to multiply its yield, and thus serve humanity.

As he progressed through his studies, eventually earning a PhD in plant pathology, Norman became increasingly interested in the plight of farmers around the world. He knew from his own experience that farming was a difficult life, but in many parts of the world, it was more than difficult—it was life-threatening. Famines, droughts, and diseases ravaged crops, leaving millions without enough to eat.

In 1944, Norman's journey took him to Mexico, where his true life's calling began to take shape on a global scale. The challenges were immense. Farmers struggled with low yields, and wheat crops were constantly ravaged by stem rust, a devastating fungal disease. But to Norman, this was no different from the tough seasons he had faced on the family farm. He rolled up his sleeves, just as he had as a boy in Iowa, and began to work the land alongside the farmers.

In Mexico, he became convinced that the problem was not just a lack of food but a lack of knowledge and opportunity. He saw how God's creation, properly nurtured, could produce abundantly, and he became determined to find ways to increase food production, even in the harshest conditions. His faith propelled him forward, even when the task seemed impossible. He believed, as his father had taught him, that perseverance and trust in God's plan would bear fruit.

He felt immense empathy toward the impoverished Mexican farmers. He wrote to his wife:

> These places I've seen have clubbed my mind—they are so poor and depressing. The earth is so lacking in life force; the plants just cling to existence. They don't really grow; they just fight to stay alive. . . . Can you imagine a poor Mexican struggling to feed his family? I don't know what we can do to help but we've got to do something.[63]

And so, after years of failure upon failure, Norman succeeded. He bred new strains of wheat that could resist disease and produce higher yields—much higher yields! "Mexican farmers had reaped about 760 pounds of wheat from every acre planted" before Norman tackled their problem—within a few decades, "the figure had risen to almost 2,500 pounds per acre—triple the harvest from the same land."[64]

His breakthrough came in the form of dwarf wheat varieties that thrived in harsh environments, producing unprecedented amounts of grain. The results were astonishing, and soon what had begun in the fields of Mexico spread across the entire world. Suddenly, countries like India and Pakistan, where famines threatened millions of lives, were able to grow thriving and healthy wheat.

In every success, Norman saw the hand of God. His innovations were not just the result of scientific ingenuity but, to him, an answer to prayer—an outgrowth of the moral duty to care for the land and for others. In a sense, Norman had never left the farm. He was still tilling the soil but now his field was the world, and his crop was hope. His crop was quite literally feeding millions of starving people.

As the Green Revolution took hold, Norman's work saved countless lives. For his efforts, he would one day be awarded the Nobel Peace Prize, but to Norman, it was never about accolades. It was about answering a higher calling. His faith had driven him to discover and create, to push beyond the limits of what seemed possible. In doing so, he fulfilled the mission his father had first set before him: to serve God and humanity through the work of his hands. Even in his Nobel lecture, Norman was careful to cite examples from scripture to demonstrate that underneath all his learning, the faith of his family was the driving force. He said, "Plant diseases, drought, desolation, despair were recurrent catastrophes during the ages" and building granaries for the future was one response, as was obvious in "Pharaoh's dreams and Joseph's interpretation of imminent famine and his preparation for it.

"For his time, Joseph was wise, with the help of his God," Norman said. "But today we should be far wiser." He encouraged the development of international granaries—suggesting that we should tackle world hunger, and not merely confine ourselves, as Joseph did, to the immediate problems of our own people.

Guided by this generous spirit, Norman concluded with this beautiful thought:

> [B]y developing and applying the scientific and technological skills of the twentieth century for "the well-being of mankind throughout the world", he may still see Isaiah's prophesies come true: "... And the desert shall rejoice, and blossom as the rose ... And the parched ground shall become a pool, and the thirsty land springs of water ..."[65]

**

God's blessings truly extend to all parts of our life, and to all types of work, from the farm to the classroom. Throughout scripture, God makes clear that our work is meant to be not just for ourselves, and not merely for Him, but for the benefit of our neighbors. Norman's love for people motivated him to great acts of innovation and change. He may have saved as many as a billion lives, and radically reduced extreme poverty in the twentieth century. It was all the more remarkable and notable that he did this at a time when another train of thought proposed that the only solution to world hunger was to reduce the number of mouths. Norman, with a love for humanity planted in his heart by humanity's Maker, largely rejected this as the primary theme of his work, instead working to increase the amount of food. He was successful beyond measure.

Judeo-Christian principles didn't just shape our justice system, our medical system, our educational system, our free market system, our social welfare systems, our legal frameworks for human rights, and even our systems of governance—they also laid the foundation for our farming and agricultural systems! These principles of reaping and sowing, with their deep emphasis on hard work, have guided every aspect of our society. From the fields to the courts, from hospitals to schools, these principles have woven themselves into the very fabric of what makes the United States of America thrive. When we choose to partner with God, there is no aspect of life that remains untouched by His transformative power.

The idea that a rural farm boy from Iowa, growing up in the early 1900s, could go on to change the world through prayer, hard work, grit and determination, and a vision aligned with God's will is the embodiment of what this country stands for. It is proof that God is not distant; He is here, present in every part of our lives. When we bring our work—no matter how simple or grand—before Him, He can use it to bring transformation on a scale we cannot imagine. The Bible reminds us in Ecclesiastes 3:1 (KJV), "To every thing there is a season, and a time for every purpose under the heaven."

Lessons Learned

"FARMING" IS ABOUT STEWARDSHIP, NOT JUST SURVIVAL. Norman Borlaug learned early on from his father that farming was about more than providing for one's family—it was about fulfilling a higher calling. Tending to the land was an act of stewardship, an opportunity to honor God by caring for His creation. This lesson is as easily applied to farming as it would be to any vocation! Replace "tending to the land" with "tending to the task at hand." It does not matter who you are or what you do; when you put your mind and your strength to a purpose, you honor God. And in return, God will honor you!

FAITH GUIDES EVERY ASPECT OF LIFE. From the fields of Iowa to the halls of the University of Minnesota to the blighted fields in Mexico and beyond, Norman's faith was the compass that guided him through every challenge. He learned that faith wasn't just something for Sundays; it was integral to his work, his studies, and his relationships. God's hand was in everything, and every endeavor—whether farming or science—was an opportunity to partner with Him.

HUMILITY IS PRACTICED IN SERVICE TO OTHERS. Norman's father taught him that their work as farmers was ultimately about serving others—feeding their neighbors and contributing to the greater good. This sense of humility and service was a cornerstone of Norman's character and later inspired his work in agricultural science. His innovations were driven by the God-given desire to alleviate hunger and help the world's most vulnerable populations.

Chapter 15

JOHN BAKER

There's No True Healing without the Church

Rick Warren wasn't looking to start a global movement when he founded Saddleback Church in 1980. He was a young man with a heart for people and a vision to reach the unchurched. But as the church grew, Rick began to realize that people weren't just showing up on Sunday mornings for a message—they were showing up broken, addicted, and weighed down by the kind of pain that can only be carried in silence. They came because they were desperate for hope, and they found in Saddleback a community that was willing to listen, love, and provide a way forward.

But something was missing. As Rick and his pastoral team prayed over their growing congregation, they began to notice a pattern. Week after week, people came through the doors. It wasn't just one person or a small group. The brokenness was pervasive, and many of those struggling felt too ashamed to talk about it. Even in the church, addiction carries a stigma. People wanted help, but they didn't know where to turn.

As the '80s progressed to the '90s, addiction in all its forms was ravaging communities. Alcoholism, drug abuse, pornography, gambling—these chains were tightening around individuals and families alike. Warren knew the church had to do more. His vision was bigger than offering a comforting message or a warm hug after the service. He wanted to see real transformation. But how? How could the church confront something as deeply ingrained and destructive as addiction?

It was in 1991 that John Baker, a recovering alcoholic and member of Saddleback, approached Warren with an idea. Baker had experienced the life-changing power of the twelve-step recovery program made famous by Alcoholics Anonymous. But as transformative as the program had been, John felt that something was missing. There was no explicit mention of Jesus Christ, the true higher power. He believed recovery needed more than just behavioral change—it necessitated spiritual renewal. Baker wrote a thirteen-page letter to Rick outlining a vision for a Christ-centered recovery program that would integrate the twelve steps with biblical principles. Warren read the letter and immediately agreed that this was the missing piece!

Saddleback launched Celebrate Recovery, a program designed to help people find freedom from all kinds of hurts, hang-ups, and habits. The focus wasn't just on addiction; it was on the root causes of pain, trauma, and brokenness. Rick and John understood that addiction was often a symptom of deeper issues, and they wanted to offer a space where people could be honest about their struggles—where they didn't have to hide.

Celebrate Recovery began with a small group of people who

gathered weekly in a modest room at Saddleback Church. They came to confess their sins, admit their failures, and—most important—find healing. From the very beginning, the program was rooted in the Gospel. Jesus was the healer, and His grace was sufficient to overcome every shackle. The group followed a structured format, working through the twelve steps, but each step was framed by scripture and grounded in faith. Step by step, week by week, people began to experience real, lasting change. Before their very eyes, lives were being transformed!

As the weeks turned into months, word began to spread. People who had once been held captive by their addictions were walking in freedom. Families that had been torn apart were being restored. The program wasn't just helping people stop self-destructive behavior—it was healing souls. It didn't take long for other churches to notice, and soon Warren and Baker were fielding calls from pastors around the country who wanted to bring Celebrate Recovery to their own congregations.

Celebrate Recovery began to grow, but the heart of the program remained the same: It was a place for broken people to encounter the grace of God in a tangible way. No matter what your issue, there was room at the table. And unlike many other programs, Celebrate Recovery was rooted in community. It wasn't just about an individual's recovery—it was about the church members coming together to lift one another up. This wasn't just a program; it was a movement of God's people walking in the light of His love and grace.

The driving force behind Celebrate Recovery was simple but profound: People in the church were hurting, and they needed more than just a sermon—they needed healing. They needed a space where they could be honest about their struggles without fear of judgment. And they needed a framework for recovery that wasn't just about self-improvement but about spiritual transformation.

Since its founding in 1991, Celebrate Recovery has grown beyond anything Rick Warren or John Baker could have imagined. It is now in over thirty-five thousand churches worldwide, helping millions of people find freedom from addiction, abuse, codependency, and countless other forms of bondage. The program has been translated into multiple languages and is used not only in churches but also in prisons, recovery centers, and community groups.

But at its core, Celebrate Recovery is still about the same thing it was about in the beginning: helping people encounter Jesus Christ, the ultimate healer. It's about walking through the dark nights of the soul together, knowing that God is with us every step of the way. It's about transforming pain into purpose and finding hope in the midst of brokenness.

In many ways, Celebrate Recovery has shifted the culture of the church. It has made space for vulnerability, for honesty, and for healing. It has shown that addiction isn't something that has to be hidden in the shadows. Instead, it can be brought into the light of God's grace, where real transformation can happen. It has also reminded the church of its calling to be a place of healing, not just for the spiritually broken but for those who are physically, mentally, and emotionally broken.

Through Celebrate Recovery, the church has stepped into her role as a beacon of hope for those who are struggling. It has shown the world that Jesus is still in the business of setting captives free. And it has reminded us all that no matter how deep our hurt, how strong our addiction, or how dark our night, God's grace is greater still. This movement has done more than just help people recover—it has restored faith in the power of the church to bring about real, lasting change.

As Rick Warren once said, "We are not a hotel for saints; we are a hospital for sinners." And through Celebrate Recovery, that vision has come to life in churches around the world. The Gospel doesn't just change hearts; it changes lives. It heals the broken, restores the lost, and makes all things new. This is the story of Celebrate Recovery—a movement born out of the felt need for healing, sustained by the power of the Gospel, and carried forward by the church as a force for good in a world that desperately needs it.

* * *

I love everything about this story! I personally know men and women whose lives have been transformed by Celebrate Recovery. I recently called Rick Warren to hear from his own lips why he and John Baker launched this transformative ministry. He shared how Celebrate Recovery was born out of a deep conviction that the church needed to offer a safe place for people to experience true healing. "We realized," Rick said, "that recovery isn't just for those battling substance abuse. It's for everyone who's struggling and needs God's grace." This was about more than just sobriety; it was about redemption and spiritual transformation, and it has since impacted millions around the globe.

What I love most about this story is that it shows the true purpose of the church. Celebrate Recovery has played a significant role in addressing the opioid crisis in our nation. I could write a whole book about how, for years, the abundance of overprescribed powerful painkillers, with people underestimating their addictive potential, led millions of Americans down a dangerous path. At the same time, porous borders have allowed illegal opioids like heroin and fentanyl to flood our communities, further exacerbating the crisis, and it's clear why the opioid epidemic has ravaged families, overwhelmed healthcare systems, and left countless lives in ruins.

But this isn't a book about blame. This is a book of stories. I believe the stories in this book act as a road map to a brighter future. When she is at her best, the church has the ability to be an agent of transformative change in our nation and the world. Celebrate Recovery is one of many examples of how the church has stepped into the gaps left by broken systems and offered hope where the world only sees despair. It's a powerful reminder that healing doesn't come from policy changes alone; it comes from a community of believers who are willing to stand in the trenches with those who are hurting.

The opioid crisis may be a vast and complex problem, but it is people like Rick Warren and ministries like Celebrate Recovery that show us the solution begins at the heart level—by offering grace, compassion, and practical help. When the church answers this call, lives are restored, families are reunited, and communities are healed. The church, in its most authentic form, becomes a beacon of hope, reminding us that even in the darkest moments, God's love can transform the seemingly impossible into stories of redemption.

Lessons Learned

WE MUST RECOGNIZE OUR NEED FOR HEALING. The church must not only preach salvation but also provide spaces for healing and restoration, addressing the pain, trauma, and brokenness within its community.

WE MUST CENTER OUR RECOVERY AROUND CHRIST. Programs like Celebrate Recovery show that true freedom and recovery come through Jesus Christ. Spiritual renewal is the key to overcoming addiction and personal struggles.

COMMUNITY IS ESSENTIAL. Recovery is not an isolated journey but one that requires the support, accountability, and love of a faith community. Churches play a vital role in walking with people through their darkest moments. And we believers must not judge those who are struggling. Instead, we must minister to them!

Chapter 16

GEORGE WASHINGTON CARVER

The Plant Doctor

From his earliest memories, George Washington Carver knew he was different. Born in the early 1860s, just before the end of the Civil War, George, along with his brother, James, lived on the farm of Moses and Susan Carver, a white family in Missouri. Moses and Susan had once "owned" George's mother, but with the ratification of the Thirteenth Amendment, their legal claim over human lives came to an end.

Though George had no memories of his first year, it was marked by extraordinary trauma. He never knew who his father was, but he heard later that he had been enslaved by a neighbor and had died in a farming accident. George also never knew his mother. While George was a still an infant, raiders stormed the Carver farm under the cover of night. During the Civil War, it was common for lawless men to roam the country looking to kidnap and resell Black people. These men, seeking profit in the chaos, kidnapped George and his mother. The raiders vanished into the darkness, leaving no trace.

Moses Carver was furious at the loss of what he still considered his "property" and hired a man to retrieve them. Weeks later, the hired man returned with baby George, weakened by whooping cough but alive. Tragically, George's mother was never found. Whether she had been sold into slavery or met a grimmer fate was a question no one could answer.

This haunting loss became the shadowy backdrop of George's early childhood. Orphaned, he would never know his parents or his family history. George had recurring whooping cough that over time gave him a weak throat and a high, thin voice. "My body was very feeble and it was a constant warfare between life and death to see who would gain the mastery." After the war brought emancipation to Missouri, George and James stayed on at the Carver household, not as slaves, but not quite as sons either. James was a "husky" boy and helped around the farm, but since George remained frail, he did easier work.

There were many happy moments, and George thought well of the Carvers in later life, though his descriptions of them didn't make it seem like they acted as substitute parents for the forlorn boys. "My brother James and I grew up together, sharing each other's sorrows on the splendid farm owned by Mr. Carver," George said, evoking both the beauty and freedom of nature and the pain and loneliness of orphanhood.

Happily, George's sorrows would also be lightened by his conversion to Christianity.

I was just a mere boy when converted, hardly ten years old. There isn't much of a story to it. God just came into my heart one afternoon while I was alone in the "loft" of our big barn while I was shelling corn to carry to the mill to be ground into meal.

A dear little white boy, one of our neighbors, about my age came by one Saturday morning and in talking and playing he told me he was going to Sunday school tomorrow morning. I was eager to know what a Sunday school was. He said they sang hymns and prayed. I asked him what prayer was and what they said. I do not remember what he said; only remember that as soon as he left I climbed up into the "loft," knelt down by the barrel of corn and prayed as best I could.

I do not remember what I said. I only recall that I felt so good that I prayed several times before I quit. My brother and myself were the only colored children in that neighborhood and of course, we could not go to church or Sunday school, or school of any kind. This was my simple conversion, and I have tried to keep the faith.[66]

Nature truly was George's refuge. Young George would crouch down, squinting at the earth, trying to see the spirit of God moving among the roots and stems. These simple lessons planted seeds in George's heart that would grow throughout his life. From an early age, George felt a special love for growing things, especially flowers. He'd spend hours—squander hours, adults thought of the distractable boy—wandering the woodlands looking at plants.

Perhaps nature also gave him an escape from bitterness. Burying himself in scripture, George embraced verses about guidance and perseverance. In the darkest moments in his life, he said, he turned to Proverbs 3:6 (KJV)—"In all thy ways acknowledge him and he shall direct thy paths"—and Philippians 4:13 (KJV)—"I can do all things through Christ which strengtheneth me."

George kept up his study of the natural world, but he learned to keep it a secret between him and God.

"Day after day I spent in the woods alone in order to collect my floral beauties," George recalled, "and put them in my little garden I had hidden in brush not far from the house, as it was considered foolishness in the neighborhood to waste time on flowers."[67]

When George wandered the woods alone, he would talk to the trees and plants as if they were old friends. He believed with all his heart that God's presence could be found everywhere—in every leaf, every stone, and every drop of rain. As he walked, George felt a profound peace settle over him, as if the very trees whispered back, affirming his words. He saw the woods not just as a collection of plants and animals but as a cathedral of God's presence, alive with His breath and purpose.

George spoke to the earth as if it could hear him, and somehow, it responded.

George's quiet brilliance set him apart. In a world where the color of his skin meant he was often treated as invisible—or worse—George's gentleness and wisdom stood in sharp contrast to the cruelty around him. The world didn't quite know what to make of him. To many, he was an oddity: a Black boy who treated plants as though they were people and walked in the woods as if conversing with God Himself.

But to those who truly knew him, George Washington Carver was nothing less than a miracle in the making, with his gift for bringing life where others saw death. George could envision a future no one had yet imagined—a future where he would heal not just fields and gardens but also lives, entire communities, and even the way the world understood science and nature.

Despite the frailty of his body, George had a mighty faith. Following what he sensed was God's calling for his life, he left home at the age of eleven or twelve, chasing after education in the schools for Black Americans that had opened during Reconstruction. He left the Carvers and began living with various families in the free Black community for the next fourteen years. One white couple whom he met after the wife was impressed by his singing in church encouraged George to apply to college.

Eventually, George's determination led him to Simpson College in Iowa. He was only just managing to support himself financially, running a laundry business and living "on prayer, beef suet, and corn meal, and quite often being without the suet and meal."[68] At Simpson, he began studying art, captivated by his love of drawing plants and nature. But his heart remained with the land, and with the encouragement of a teacher who saw his potential, he transferred to Iowa Agricultural College, becoming its first Black student, to study botany and agriculture. At the college, George's gentle genius truly bloomed, and his path became a calling.

George excelled in botany and soil science, uncovering the mysteries of the soil with the same reverence he had once reserved for the woods near the Carver farm. As he studied, he felt God's hand guiding him. In those quiet laboratories and sunlit fields, George realized that his life's purpose was much more than the pursuit of knowledge; it was a path of healing—healing soil, healing communities, and healing generations trapped in cycles of poor crops and poverty.

He'd become known as the "Plant Doctor." George Washington Carver revolutionized Southern agriculture by introducing pioneering crop rotation techniques and creating innovative applications for alternative crops like peanuts, sweet potatoes, and soybeans. In the late nineteenth and early twentieth centuries, the Southern United States faced a serious agricultural crisis: Years of continuous cotton cultivation had severely depleted the soil, leaving farmers with poor yields and limited options. Recognizing this, George devised a sustainable system of crop rotation to restore soil health.

George advocated for planting nitrogen-fixing crops—such as peanuts, legumes, and soybeans—which naturally enriched the soil by restoring essential nutrients. By rotating these crops with cotton, farmers could regenerate their land and increase its productivity. But George's vision went further than soil restoration! He realized that to make this new approach economically viable, farmers would need profitable markets for these alternative crops.

George's approach was holistic: He saw the connection between environmental health, economic resilience, and community wellbeing. Through his tireless advocacy, he educated farmers across the South, showing them not only how to revive their land but also how to thrive. George Washington Carver's legacy remains a cornerstone of sustainable agriculture, illustrating how innovative farming techniques can uplift entire communities while preserving the environment for future generations. His contributions fundamentally transformed Southern farming practices and had a lasting impact on American agriculture.

George believed that the Bible held wisdom about the natural world and often referenced scriptures that spoke of God's provision through plants, soil, and stewardship. He once explained, "I love to think of nature as an unlimited broadcasting station through which God speaks to us every hour, if we will only tune in." To him, studying plants was like studying God's own blueprint for creation, and it was this reverent dependence on God that directed his hands and mind.

The love and wonder with which God blessed George also strengthened his ability to move beyond the difficulties of his childhood. In later years, as a respected scientist, when someone asked him how he was able to overcome, he gave eloquent life advice.

> *Bitterness poisons our systems and drives the Christ out of us. It puts us into the position of an eye for an eye and a tooth for a tooth. When you get in touch with the great creative power you just cannot get bitter because there is so much of beauty, so much of sublimity in the world that you can't waste your time getting bitter.*[69]

* * *

Proverbs 14:34 (ESV) tells us, "Righteousness exalts a nation, but sin is a reproach to any people." George Washington Carver embodied this truth, choosing righteousness even when the weight of his past could have easily led him down a different path. He faced profound pain and injustice from a young age and could have been left with scars that could have defined his entire life. Yet he refused to dwell on the cruelty he had suffered and instead sought to live by a higher standard—one rooted in his faith. Carver focused his energy on helping others, believing that his talents and knowledge were gifts from God meant to be shared. In choosing to let go of resentment, he dedicated himself to lifting others up, particularly the poor farmers struggling to make a living from depleted land. His faith guided him to see the potential in everything—from the soil underfoot to the human spirit—reminding us that righteousness is not only a choice but also a way of life that can transform the lives of those around us.

As a nation, we've faced trials that tested these values, and at times, we have fallen short. But throughout our history, those same values have continually called us back to our moral compass, reminding us that true greatness is found in humility, service, and faithfulness. "If my people, who are called by my name, will humble themselves and pray and seek my face and turn from their wicked ways, then I will hear from heaven, and I will forgive their sin and will heal their land" (2 Chronicles 7:14). That verse speaks to our national calling, as relevant today as it was at our founding.

I believe America needs to return to the wellspring of our faith. We are called to be a city upon a hill (Matthew 5:14), a beacon of hope and righteousness. If we stay grounded in these enduring values, America will continue to be that light—not by turning away from our heritage, but by embracing it fully. Through every trial, we must stand firm in the knowledge that these principles have not only defined us; they are what will sustain us.

George Washington Carver's life shows us what it means to choose righteousness over resentment. In his unwavering dedication to his faith and his mission, he transformed not only his own life but also the lives of countless others. By letting go of bitterness and focusing on serving those in need, he became a living example of the power of faith to enable us to overcome even the deepest injustices. His legacy reminds us that a life rooted in righteousness, humility, and service can light the way forward for both individuals and nations alike, proving that true greatness is built on the bedrock of faith and resilience.

Lessons Learned

FAITH AND RESILIENCE TRANSFORM PAIN INTO PURPOSE. George Washington Carver's early life was marked by profound loss and injustice. Yet instead of succumbing to bitterness or resentment, he chose to focus on his faith and let it guide his actions. George found a higher purpose in serving others through his talents. George's decision to resist bitterness doesn't mean that the loss and injustice he suffered as a young man were unreal or unimportant. Rather, George's choice was that he wouldn't let those experiences define him. It's easy to let anger and bitterness become so all-consuming that they poison life's joys and make it impossible for us to build a different world for others. Moving forward means looking forward in forgiveness.

TRUE GREATNESS LIES IN SERVICE AND STEWARDSHIP. George's approach to life and work demonstrated a deep understanding of stewardship—whether it was nurturing plants, restoring soil, or uplifting struggling farmers. When he became a teacher at Booker T. Washington's school, the Tuskegee Institute in Alabama, he developed a sterling reputation as a mentor for young people. In one of his lectures, he emphasized the importance of committing deeply to the study of God's world. "A person is never completely educated; he only becomes an artist in the things he knows," George said. "Interest and ability are the only limitations on knowledge; the more one knows, the wider he is known and the more useful is his life."

VALUE AND DIGNITY ARE FOUND THROUGH CONNECTION WITH GOD AND CREATION. George's life was a testament to the transformative power of seeing every aspect of life—plants, soil, and people—as valuable and sacred. For George, this started with the flowers. He said, "I remember as a boy a little expression that has lingered with me all through life. It said, 'that flowers were the sweetest thing that God ever made and forgot to put a soul into it.' It was one of the things that impressed me so very much that I always remembered it, but as I grow older and study plant life, I am convinced that God didn't forget to do anything that was worthwhile."[70]

Chapter 17

FRANCIS SCOTT KEY

America's Story Is Still Being Written

September 14, 1814, 1:00 a.m.

The thunderous booms from the cannons reverberated through every fiber of Francis Scott Key's being, shaking the very deck beneath his feet. Helpless and overwhelmed, he stood perfectly still, his heart pounding with a mix of fear and unwavering determination for his countrymen. He watched as Fort McHenry, the symbol of American resilience, was mercilessly decimated. Nineteen British ships unleashed their fury upon the fort, unloading every ounce of firepower they possessed. The air was thick with the acrid smell of smoke and gunpowder, forcing Francis to shield his nose and mouth with a kerchief.

Amid the chaos, fires blazed throughout the fort, casting dancing shadows that flickered in the dense haze. Francis, a man driven by his deep sense of patriotism, had embarked on this treacherous journey to negotiate the release of his dear friend Dr. William Beanes, who had been captured by the British a month prior. William had dared to stand up to British soldiers, causing trouble, and in retaliation, the British had imprisoned him belowdecks in the brig of a ship anchored in the Chesapeake Bay.

The sheer magnitude of the onslaught was staggering. The relentless barrage of cannonballs hurtling toward the harbor left Francis breathless. The British had unleashed a force rarely witnessed in their storied history. From dusk till the early morning hours, the thunderous booms continued unabated, drowning out the anguished cries of the men, women, and children within the fort. *How long can this continue?* The thought had formed hours earlier and still consumed his mind. *How long before the entire fort has been wiped from the face of the earth? How long could anyone last against such an onslaught?*

The United States of America, with its eighteen states standing on the precipice of destiny, was a country born and forged in the crucible of war. Its people had known little respite from the battles that shaped their nation. Yet despite its imperfections and challenges, Francis wholeheartedly believed in the potential of America. His faith in God and unyielding belief in the American people were the bedrock of his conviction. He knew that if given the chance to flourish, the United States would someday become a beacon of light, illuminating the world with its undeniable beauty and boundless possibilities. The stakes were high, and America's success was paramount.

Francis's eyes were fixed on the mammoth flag once again being hoisted by the men at the fort. The flag rose slowly, framed by smoke and flames. Commissioned by Major George Armistead, it was a colossal masterpiece measuring an impressive thirty by forty-two feet. It bore fifteen stripes and fifteen stars, with each star stretching nearly two feet from point to point.[71] The flag symbolized the hopes and dreams of a fledgling nation, acting as a tangible representation of the sacrifices made and the ideals fought for. Its presence served as a rallying point for both soldiers and civilians, embodying the spirit of perseverance and the promise of a brighter future.

This flag had fallen from sight numerous times throughout the attack. More than once, it had been hit directly. Each time it fell, the British erupted in victorious cheers. Yet every time it disappeared, a man would emerge through the smoke and haze, clutching the remnants of the tattered flag to raise it again, as if it were a phoenix rising from the ashes. The fires that raged within the fort transformed the act of hoisting the United States flag into a sight that bordered on the mystical and the sacred, the shadows of the rising flag dancing in the haze. This undying symbol of hope and resilience reinforced Francis's belief that America's destiny was not just a dream but an achievable reality.

"All they need do is take the flag down." Major General Robert Ross, the ship's captain, had arrived without Francis's noticing. "I have been clear that if they stop raising the flag, we will stop our attack. And still, they persist. I'll give it to you Americans; you've got more grit and determination, more stubbornness than any people I've heard of."

Francis tore his eyes from the flag and locked eyes with Ross. This man had demanded that Francis and William Beanes stay on the ship until after the attack. "You won't break them." Francis's voice was grim. "They aren't fighting the British empire, nor any specific enemy."

The major general offered a curious look. "I don't understand," he said. "What do you mean?"

"We are not who it is that attacks us. We care not what flag flies above your mast. The men of Fort McHenry are fighting for a new world. They are fighting for generations to come. They are fighting for a future that their children's children could scarcely dream of."

Ross placed a hand on Francis's shoulder. "No one, no matter how deep and abiding their faith, can withstand the full force of the British army. Your countrymen are valiant but will surrender before the sun reaches its zenith."

Francis smiled sadly. "You aren't hearing me," he said. "If need be, every last man in that fort would give his life for the idea that is the United States of America. I know those men—those families. You will not break them."

Francis turned away from the carnage. He needed to update his friend. He had been permitted to move about the ship as he wished, but while the negotiations for the release of William Beanes had gone well, both men had been told they were not allowed to leave the ship until after the battle. William was to stay in the brig until the attack was complete.

As Francis passed the guard and walked down the dark, narrow stairs, he made his way to the brig. When he arrived, he found William on his knees in prayer. The moment William caught sight of Francis, he sprang to his feet, leaning eagerly against the iron bars. "Does it still stand?" he asked, breathless with anticipation. "Does the flag still fly?"

Francis shook his head in wonderment, his voice filled with awe and admiration. "It has been torn to shreds," he replied, "but it still flies. The men at Fort McHenry will not allow it to fall."

Francis Scott Key was not a warrior; he was a lawyer, a writer, a believer in the faithfulness of God. When he found himself back on deck an hour later, witnessing his compatriots courageously battling against insurmountable odds, a surge of inspiration welled within him. He began to weave words, penning a poem, a song that encapsulated the spirit of the moment.[72] The words he etched upon the page would become the anthem of a great nation, resonating through the ages.

> O say, can you see, by the dawn's early light,
> What so proudly we hailed at the twilight's last gleaming,
> Whose broad stripes and bright stars, through the perilous fight,
> O'er the ramparts we watched were so gallantly streaming?
> And the rocket's red glare, the bombs bursting in the air,
> Gave proof through the night that our flag was still there;
> O say, does that star-spangled banner yet wave
> O'er the land of the free and the home of the brave?

Something I had not noticed until recently is that our national anthem, "The Star-Spangled Banner," ends with a question mark. For generations, Americans have sung the song with an exclamation point—"O say, does that star-spangled banner yet wave / O'er the land of the free and the home of the brave!" However, Francis Scott Key wrote the poem before he knew the end of the story. The question was real! Did the flag still fly?

***

Today, when I look around our great country, I see a lot of question marks. Though there is no cannon fire in the battles we face, we are in the midst of an entirely different kind of battle. Similarly to those involved in the battle of Fort McHenry, we are in a battle for the heart and soul of the United States of America. And in the midst of any struggle, the outcome is unclear.

Francis Scott Key spoke with surety. He knew to the core of his being that the men of Fort McHenry would not give up. He understood their determination and devotion. What remained unclear was whether any of them would be left alive, and whether the fledgling country could survive such an onslaught.

There are real question marks in our world today. We face real battles, and I don't for a second downplay any of them. Yet we have something Francis Scott Key did not. As I type these words, it is July 5, 2024. Last night, I sat with my beautiful fiancée and my family, and we enjoyed fireworks in the greatest nation on earth. As a nation, we have almost 250 years of history to look back on. We have almost 250 years of seeing God's faithfulness, of seeing the movements of the Holy Spirit.

The story of Francis Scott Key and the battle of Fort McHenry is one of literally tens of thousands of stories of God's faithfulness, of the grit and determination of the American people. I am writing this book in part to remind us who we are. The men and women who came before us laid a firm foundation. Do not lose heart! Do not let the question marks replace the exclamation points!

Yes, the battle is real. But take heart and do not be afraid. God is moving today, and miracles are still taking place. In our times of uncertainty, we have the advantage of looking back at our history and witnessing the countless moments where faith, perseverance, and divine intervention brought us through. Just as Francis Scott Key looked upon the flag at dawn and saw a symbol of resilience and hope, we, too, can look at our nation's history and see the fingerprints of God guiding us.

As we move forward, let us remember the lessons of our past. Let us hold fast to the faith that has carried us through the darkest nights. Let us be inspired by the bravery of those who fought for freedom and justice. And let us continue to build on the foundation they laid, confident that with God's guidance, we can face any challenge and emerge stronger. Our story is still being written, and each of us has a role to play in shaping the future. Let us rise to the occasion with faith, hope, and unwavering determination.

Lessons Learned

FAITH AND RESILIENCE ARE FOUNDATIONAL TO OVERCOMING CHALLENGES. In the story of Francis Scott Key witnessing the battle at Fort McHenry, the unwavering faith of the soldiers and their determination to keep the flag flying exemplify the strength needed to endure in times of trial. Despite overwhelming odds, their resilience became a symbol of hope. Like those at Fort McHenry, we must hold fast to our faith when faced with adversity.

GOD'S FAITHFULNESS IS EVIDENT THROUGHOUT HISTORY. America has a history of resilience! We now have almost 250 years of witnessing God's faithfulness. Whether in the battle of Fort McHenry or in countless other moments, divine intervention and the grit of the American people have carried our nation through difficult times. The same faith and perseverance that guided those who came before will guide us through today's challenges.

OUR NATION'S STORY IS STILL BEING WRITTEN, AND WE ALL HAVE A PART TO PLAY! Just as the soldiers and Francis Scott Key played their roles in shaping the course of America's history, we, too, are part of the ongoing story. By holding fast to our faith and remembering the lessons of the past, we can rise to meet the challenges of today, confident that we are building on a firm foundation laid by those who came before us. When Francis wrote the words to what would one day become our national anthem, he did so in the midst of battle, not knowing the outcome. The question mark at the end of "The Star-Spangled Banner" reflects this uncertainty. Similarly, in our lives and our nation's struggles, outcomes can be unclear, but faith in God and in the principles that guide us gives us strength to persevere through the unknown.

Chapter 18

HEROES WILL RISE IN A CRISIS

Yesterday, I boarded a helicopter at McEntire Joint National Guard Base in Richland County, South Carolina, with members of the National Guard. We needed a bird's-eye view of the devastation left in the wake of Hurricane Helene, which had come out of the gulf as a monstrous Category 4 storm just days earlier. The power of the storm was still fresh in our minds, but seeing it from the air—flattened homes, flooded streets, and the endless stretch of destruction—was beyond sobering.

This was not the first time South Carolina has endured such devastation. As I flew over the wreckage left by Hurricane Helene, my mind flashed back to another disaster from 2015. Then, I took to the air to assess the damage from the "thousand-year flood," a once-in-a-millennium event that ravaged portions of the state. Record rainfall led to catastrophic flooding—dams burst, rivers overflowed, and entire towns were swallowed by water. Nineteen lives were lost, and the damages reached into the billions of dollars. The scale of destruction I saw now felt eerily familiar.

Helene was a storm of historic proportions, and when it made landfall, its winds were roaring at speeds of up to 140 miles per hour, tearing apart homes, uprooting trees, and snapping power lines. The sheer force of the storm left the region in ruins.

As Helene struck the coastline, the surge of water it carried was just as fearsome as its winds. The storm surge in some areas climbed as high as fourteen feet, inundating entire neighborhoods and swallowing cars, homes, and businesses under a fast-moving wall of water. North Carolina, South Carolina, Florida, and Georgia were among the hardest hit, with vulnerable areas completely overwhelmed. Streets turned into rivers, and residents found themselves trapped, waiting for rescue teams to pull them from their flooded homes.

Rainfall was relentless as Helene stalled over the region, unleashing more than twenty inches of rain in some areas. Rivers swelled far beyond their banks, cutting off entire towns as floodwaters surged. The sheer volume of rain overwhelmed drainage systems, leaving cities submerged for days. Flash floods tore through inland communities, catching many off guard as the waters rose with frightening speed. As of today, 49 residents of South Carolina have lost their lives, and more than 230 Americans have perished in the aftermath of the storm. As the days go on, it seems inevitable that this tragic number will rise.

The further we flew, the more difficult it became to comprehend the vast scale of the devastation. Each shattered home represented a family torn apart, and each abandoned vehicle was a symbol of the daily lives and routines that had been suddenly and violently disrupted. Everywhere we looked, we saw remnants of lives upended, communities where friends, neighbors, and churches once thrived that may never look the same again. In the aftermath of disasters like Hurricane Helene, you quickly realize that the true first responders aren't the government agencies. They are neighbors, churches, civilian pilots, and boat captains—ordinary people stepping up to do extraordinary things. Stories of heroism have emerged from every town and community hit by Helene.

The Bible reminds us that "weeping may stay for the night, but rejoicing comes in the morning" (Psalms 30:5), and Hurricane Helene has certainly tested our endurance. But even amid the devastation, there have been powerful stories of hope and resilience. One of the most remarkable is how Christians, united in faith, have come together from different churches to help those in need.

Seacoast Church, for example, played a pivotal role in rescuing three ninety-year-old women who were trapped in the mountains with no food, no water, and no way to communicate. Through their relationship with a civilian who owned a private helicopter, Seacoast helped deliver these people to safety. In moments like these, you see faith in action—Americans stepping up to be the miracle for their neighbors, showing the love of Christ through their actions.

Seacoast Church is just one example of a first responder. In the wake of the storm, they mobilized quickly, not waiting for official rescue teams but leading with their hearts and hands. Seacoast partnered with organizations such as Convoy of Hope, Samaritan's Purse, and other local churches to bring assistance to the hardest-hit areas. They have contributed $500,000 to various disaster relief efforts, like providing clean water, food, and emergency supplies. Seacoast volunteers gathered supplies, opened shelters, and to date have provided more than twelve thousand meals to those left stranded. Their members were not just bystanders—they were on the front lines, delivering practical hope to communities in need.

Another incredible group on the ground is Water Mission, which has been at the forefront of providing life-saving resources to devastated communities. Known for their expertise in water purification, Water Mission quickly deployed their teams to areas cut off from clean drinking water due to the storm's impact. In places like Asheville, North Carolina, where flooding had severely compromised the local water infrastructure, Water Mission set up mobile water filtration systems capable of filtering four thousand gallons of water per day. This clean water has been a lifeline for families who lost access to safe drinking water in the immediate aftermath of the storm.

Water Mission's work didn't stop there. They collaborated with local churches, including Seacoast Church, to ensure that these filtration systems were strategically placed where the need was greatest. Their efforts have helped prevent waterborne illnesses, ensuring that thousands of displaced residents have access to clean, safe water during the most critical days of recovery.

Water Mission has also been coordinating with other disaster relief organizations, including Convoy of Hope and Samaritan's Purse, to provide a holistic approach to recovery. Together, they are not only meeting the physical needs of the affected communities but also bringing hope and comfort to those who have lost so much. Whether by ensuring clean water or providing emergency supplies, these organizations are the hands and feet of Christ in a time of overwhelming need.

* * *

There has been a lot of talk and grumblings about the failures of FEMA (the Federal Emergency Management Agency). While there have indeed been some glaring shortcomings, I don't believe all of them can be attributed to FEMA. In times of disaster, the official response process can be broken, and Hurricane Helene has revealed the limitations of that system. By design, each state is responsible for managing the initial response to natural disasters. For South Carolina, that responsibility falls to my friend Governor Henry McMaster, who coordinates disaster relief efforts across the state's counties.

While the frustration with the slow and in some cases nonexistent response of FEMA is understandable, the nature of this system means that FEMA cannot be a "first responder." In fact, it typically takes a few days for FEMA to be mobilized effectively. As reports and requests for aid filter upward from local governments to the state and then to the federal level, valuable time is lost. This isn't necessarily due to inefficiency; it's simply the way the process is structured. There's an argument to be made that this process is broken and needs reform, but under current regulations, FEMA shouldn't be held solely responsible for delays. The bureaucratic chain of command ensures that federal resources are slower to arrive than what local communities need in the critical hours immediately following a disaster.

Even if the system operated as smoothly as possible, no government agency, no matter how well-oiled, can replace the true first responders. These everyday citizens rise to the occasion. This is where the church and the broader community step in. In the hours and days after Hurricane Helene hit, FEMA wasn't first on the scene; it was neighbors helping neighbors, churches mobilizing volunteers, and small businesses providing food and shelter. Faith communities, in particular, have been instrumental in providing immediate relief to those in desperate need. This is where faith becomes a miracle. Faith finds its traction not in waiting for official aid, but in stepping up and being the answer to someone else's prayer. It's through the everyday actions of ordinary people that hope is restored, and the actual work of recovery begins.

This spirit of community and quick action is what defines true resilience. Whether by clearing debris from roads, providing a warm meal, or offering a word of encouragement, these everyday heroes remind us that even in the darkest times, there are always lights shining. In the wake of Hurricane Helene, these lights came from the neighbors who stepped up, the churches that opened their doors, and the volunteers who worked tirelessly to remind us that we're never truly alone in the storm. They embody what it means to love your neighbor, to serve without hesitation, and to be the hands and feet of Christ when disaster strikes.

As a United States Senator, I work primarily in Washington, D.C., where I strive to forge policy and create legislation that serves the American people. However, since the hurricane, my phone has not stopped ringing. People are trapped, and communities are calling out for help. They need resources, and they need them fast. The requests have been overwhelming: Some towns desperately need Starlink to restore communication to cut-off areas; others need generators to power critical infrastructure or clean water to prevent the spread of disease. The needs are as varied as the communities themselves, but the one constant is the urgency of the situation.

Even as I am in the midst of crafting policy, my heart remains in my home state, with the people affected. This is where local and faith communities truly shine. In the days and weeks after a disaster like Helene, we don't wait for government agencies to catch up—we take action. Churches become shelters, kitchens become community hubs, and neighbors become rescuers. It's in these moments that our faith, our resilience, and our commitment to one another are put to the test. And each and every time, we rise to meet the challenge.

The overwhelming response to Helene is a reminder that while legislation and government programs are essential for long-term recovery, the immediate response—the first wave of hope—comes from the community. We are never truly alone in the storm. Every day, men and women step in to serve, demonstrating that resilience is not just about surviving but about standing together no matter how hard the storm is raging. America's greatness has always been found in her people—the men and women who, grounded in faith, step up when times are darkest.

Every day, we are witnessing new stories of resilience and hope, a reflection of the values woven into the fabric of this nation—at a staggering level. At the heart of this response were small business owners who provided shelter, church volunteers who organized rescue missions, and individuals who, without being asked, opened their homes and hearts to those displaced by the storm. These are the people who, regardless of recognition, are the true heroes among us. The response to Helene wasn't just about emergency aid—it was about embodying the love of Christ and reflecting the light of God's compassion.

Judeo-Christian principles have not only underpinned America's legal and political systems but have also deeply influenced her social dynamics, emphasizing love for one's neighbor and service to the greater good. This spirit is what leads ordinary men and women to extraordinary acts, inspired by the belief that we are all stewards of God's creation and responsible for one another. This sense of moral duty, anchored in faith, enables people to rise during crises, offering hope and making tangible differences in the lives of others.

As a public servant, I often find myself reflecting on how best to support the needs of the American people through legislation and policy. But in times like these, it becomes clear that no government policy or program can replace the power of community, faith, and the everyday American citizen. The true strength of this nation lies not in Washington, D.C., but in the hands of people across the country who, motivated by a higher calling, step up and take action.

This is where the core of Judeo-Christian values shines the brightest. These values have shaped not just America's institutions but her very soul. The faith that compels us to love and serve one another has laid the foundation for communities that are resilient, generous, and unshakable in times of crisis. When everyday citizens embody these principles, they create ripples of positive change that echo far beyond the immediate impact—echoes in eternity, as their actions and sacrifices leave a lasting imprint on the world.

America's greatness isn't found in her wealth or power but in our people and their faith-driven service to one another. True leadership and heroism, as demonstrated in the aftermath of Hurricane Helene, come not from positions of power but from hearts filled with compassion and conviction. These are the values that will continue to guide us through the storms and shape our nation's future for generations to come.

Lessons Learned

FAITH IN ACTION IS OUR GREATEST ASSET IN THE FACE OF DEVASTATION. It's not government systems that step up first—it's the people driven by their faith. Whether it's churches opening their doors, neighbors checking on each other, or volunteers clearing debris, everyday heroes rise because of the deep-rooted belief that serving others is a divine calling.

RESILIENCE IS BUILT ON COMMUNITY. True resilience is found in the strength of the community. While FEMA and governmental agencies play a crucial role in long-term recovery, the immediate response to disasters like Hurricane Helene comes from people banding together. Communities united by shared values of love, service, and sacrifice become unstoppable forces of recovery, proving that together, we can overcome even the most devastating storms.

JUDEO-CHRISTIAN VALUES UNDERPIN AMERICA'S DISASTER RESPONSE. The foundation of America's moral and social framework—Judeo-Christian values—guides the nation's most powerful responses to crises. These values compel ordinary citizens to do extraordinary things, stepping up to meet the needs of those around them. It's these principles that inspire selflessness, compassion, and a sense of duty that extends far beyond any governmental program.

Chapter 19

DAVID GREEN

God Has a Plan for Our Work

It was a crisp, dry day in August when there was a knock on the woman's door.

Running to the porch, the woman was delighted to see the happy face of Marie Green peering in through the glass in the door. Marie was the pastor's wife, a woman with an easy smile and bright red hair. Her family background was German, which translated into a matter-of-fact friendliness and a strict personal modesty. Even though it was the 1940s, she wore long dresses and no makeup, but her beauty shone through all the same.

Marie didn't waste much time on pleasantries before bundling one such dress into the woman's hands. "I thought you might enjoy this," she said. "It's nothing special, but the pattern is nice."

The dress was a blue—old-fashioned, and not new, but better than anything the woman had had in years. The woman couldn't find words. How had Marie even known she'd pawned her last dress the week before? She was hit with a wave of confused feelings—gratitude, embarrassment. "Oh, Mrs. Green, I couldn't."

Marie shook her head firmly and laughed. "I have plenty more at home. You're just helping me clean out my closet. Don't you go denying me the blessing of giving, now."

Later that day, Marie returned home, toting a bag of potatoes the woman had insisted she take. Maybe, Marie thought, there would be another dress in the church donation pile in a month or two. This latest gift had reduced the number of dresses in her closet from its usual three down to two. She never seemed to have more than that. *But*, she thought, *that is more than enough. What a blessing that God has given me enough to provide for others.*

Generosity defined the life of Marie Green. One of the first things her son David remembered about his childhood was the doilies. Marie used to make them in her free time, her well-practiced fingers drawing thread back and forth with a crochet hook, producing simple, pretty doilies to sell. With the small income this business made, she could contribute on her own to missionary charities.

The practice said a lot about Marie and the Green family in general. She and her husband donated to missionary work from his income, but she wanted to donate herself, from something she made, as a matter of principle. This meant even more since money was always short in the Green family as David grew up. David's father, Walter, was a pastor working for churches across the American Southwest, serving tiny congregations everywhere from Arizona to Oklahoma. Every two years, the family would move, meaning that David went to eight different schools before he graduated high school.

"Small towns, small churches, and small incomes defined our lives," he'd remember later, "making it a constant challenge for our parents to care for our family of eight."

Since the family was usually in a two-bedroom house, David and his brother would often sleep in the kitchen on a bed that could be stored away. He'd wake early to the smells of coffee brewing and eggs sizzling as his mother bustled around. Breakfast—in fact, every meal—was set by whatever his father's congregation decided to donate to the weekly food pantry. There'd be vegetables and fruit—less often, meat. Sometimes weeks would go by without meat.

His parents never let their six children feel sorry for themselves. Even though the family could never afford a car, Marie and Walter emphasized that God had given all their kids two feet—sufficient to carry them wherever they needed to go. Faith was central to the Green family's life. In fact, Walter and Marie had first met at a tent meeting. The rhythm of revivals was as natural to them as the regular monsoon seasons that swept over the desert and plains. Three times a week, the Green kids were in church, not just because their father was a preacher but because faith was seen as the center of their lives. Walter and Marie took faith so seriously that they wouldn't even let their children believe in Santa Claus, worrying that they would see this as evidence of deceitful parents and foolish support of fairy tales.

David's father was from an English background, and with that came a strong reserve. He was from a generation of men who rarely expressed their affection. As a result, David found himself mostly influenced by his mother's open, giving personality. She tried not to play favorites, but it was plain early on that he was special to her.

"I was able to make her laugh no matter what else was going on," he wrote later.

But surprisingly, he was also the problem child. His grades were so bad that he only barely made it out of high school and had to repeat the seventh grade. He hated the abstract nature of mathematical reasoning, and spent his classes daydreaming, gazing out the window at the bright sun. His lucky break was that his school offered a work-study program, whereby he could get credit by doing work in the real world. "I died and went to heaven," he remembered, excited to chase a calling that was outside school.[73]

When he turned fourteen, David took his first job as a stock boy in a local five-and-dime—McLellan's, in Altus, Oklahoma. Though he was only a teenager, he approached the work with a seriousness beyond his years. He stocked every shelf and greeted every customer with the intention of glorifying God. He quickly learned that even the smallest tasks could be done with integrity and that excellence in work was a form of worship.

David loved this experience of working in retail. Over the next few years, something began to form deep within him—a vision of what could be. He was fascinated by the way stores operated and how products moved from warehouses to shelves and into the hands of customers. His mind began to fill with ideas about how businesses could run more efficiently, but it was the way people were treated in the marketplace that captured his heart most.

There, he found his calling. In David's family, the idea of a calling was very particular. It referred to church work, and nothing else. This meant that at first, he felt confused over why he was so excited to work in a secular job, far from the hymns and sermons of his parents' lives. But he felt in his bones that this work wasn't "low or unimportant" but rather a form of honoring God with his talents.

As David rose through the ranks in local retail, he would recount his accomplishments to his mother. She always listened, and when he'd tell her about another promotion, she'd immediately ask, "What have you done for the Lord lately?"

Ruefully, David thought, *I could have been elected president and she'd still ask, "What have you done for the Lord lately?"*

Though he hemmed and hawed about it at first, he learned to value the question, because it would become his guiding light. "My mother gave me a heavenly perspective," he said. "She gave me eyes to see the difference between what carries temporal significance and what carries eternal worth.... My mom taught me discernment."[74]

This would serve him well as he achieved dreams he could never have imagined. Who could have imagined, waking every morning in the kitchen, stowing his bed away, hoping there'd be meat on the table today, that he'd achieve greatness?

Like his mother, David believed that every interaction, whether with employees or customers, was an opportunity to demonstrate Christian values in action. It was this belief that would guide him throughout his life, shaping the kind of business he would one day build.

Despite David's early passion for business, his path was not an easy one. His family struggled to make ends meet, and college was never a serious consideration. He knew he would have to find his own way in the world, relying on the work ethic instilled in him by his parents and his unwavering faith that God had a plan for his life. After marrying his high school sweetheart,

Barbara, David continued to work in retail, moving up the ranks in management. But the dream of starting his own business never left him.

In 1970, David took a leap of faith. With a $600 loan and a God-sized dream, he and Barbara started assembling miniature picture frames in their garage, working late into the night after their children had gone to bed. The hours were long, and the work was hard, but David never wavered in his belief that God was guiding their steps. He remembered his father's lessons about trusting God to provide and leaned into his faith during the difficult moments when success seemed far off.

What started as a small family project grew into something bigger than David had ever imagined. The picture frames they crafted in their garage became the foundation for what would eventually become Hobby Lobby, a chain of arts-and-crafts stores that would span the nation. From the very beginning, David was determined that his business would be different. It would not just be a way to make money but an enterprise run on biblical principles—a place where employees were treated with dignity, where customers felt valued, and where integrity guided every decision.

Hobby Lobby was built on the belief that business in general is a ministry, and David took that ministry seriously. He was committed to honoring God through the way he treated his employees, paying them well above the minimum wage and offering benefits that were unheard-of in the retail industry at the time. He also made the bold decision to close his stores on Sundays, forgoing millions of dollars in revenue each year, so that his employees could have a day of rest and time with their families in alignment with the Sabbath. This decision, rooted in his faith, baffled many in the business world, but for David, it was nonnegotiable. God came first, and if that meant sacrificing profits, so be it.

* * *

What began with David Green assembling picture frames in his garage with his wife eventually grew into a retail empire. Today, Hobby Lobby operates over a thousand stores across the United States. David's vision of running a business rooted in biblical principles has not only redefined what it means to be a successful entrepreneur but has also transformed countless lives. Over the years, the Green family has given away hundreds of millions of dollars to various Christian ministries, charities, and media initiatives. Their giving has touched every corner of Christian outreach, from education to entertainment to spreading the Gospel in innovative and unprecedented ways.

Hobby Lobby's success has been nothing short of remarkable. Today, the company generates more than $7 billion in revenue annually, and it employs over forty-six thousand people.[75] Despite its enormous growth, David Green's values have never wavered. The company continues to close its doors on Sundays, allowing employees to rest and spend time with their families. It was an audacious decision when it was first made, one that many critics thought would harm the business. However, this choice has become a hallmark of the company's commitment to living out its faith.

Hobby Lobby's employees are also paid well above industry standards, and they benefit from generous health and retirement plans. This level of care and respect for workers is a direct reflection of the Greens' belief that every individual is made in the image of God and should be treated with dignity. It's another way that their faith permeates the business—through actions, not just words.

David Green has often said that he doesn't view himself as the owner of Hobby Lobby but rather as a steward of what God has entrusted to him. This mindset, deeply rooted in his faith, has allowed him to see his wealth not as something to hoard but as something to give away. His goal, he has said many times, is to "leave the world with nothing," ensuring that everything he has been given is used to further the cause of Christ. This belief has shaped not only his life but also the lives of his children and grandchildren, and the generations of Christians who have been blessed by his generosity.

I have never had the honor of meeting David Green, although I have had the privilege of meeting his equally impressive son Steve on a handful of occasions. Each time, I have walked away inspired by the Greens' unwavering commitment to faith, family, and the success of Hobby Lobby. But it wasn't until I began writing this chapter that I truly understood the depth of their story and its humble beginnings. The tale of traveling preacher Walter Green—a man who served multiple congregations across small rural towns, pouring his heart into his ministry and leaving a lasting legacy of faith for his children—resonates deeply with me.

You may have noticed that throughout this book, I frequently revisit the stories of those who came before—the fathers, mothers, and grandparents who paved the way for the individuals we recognize today. I believe this is because no story truly stands alone. Our lives are not contained within the years we live but are part of a much larger narrative, one that began long before we arrived and will continue long after we are gone. Our values, our faith, and the choices we make ripple through time, touching the lives of future generations.

Yet I don't believe David Green's story is all that rare. I could easily have told the same story about Truett Cathy, the founder of Chick-fil-A; James Cash Penney, the founder of JCPenney; Mary Kay Ash, the founder of Mary Kay Cosmetics; Henry Parsons Crowell, the founder of Quaker Oats; and David Steward, the founder of World Wide Technology. And the list goes on and on. From the very first businesses formed in our nation's earliest days, Judeo-Christian values have provided the foundation for countless successful enterprises. These values—honesty, integrity, treating others with respect, and a commitment to hard work—are as integral to the American economy as the industries themselves.

Judeo-Christian principles undergird many thriving enterprises and successful ventures in the story of the United States of America. Whether it's a small family business or a multibillion-dollar corporation, these values serve as the moral compass that guides our leaders in the way they treat employees, serve their customers, and give back to the community. This foundation of faith is interwoven into the very fabric of the greatest American businesses. For David Green and countless others, success has never been solely about profit. It has always been about stewardship—taking what God has given and using it to make the world a better place. In this way, these business leaders remind us that commerce, when built on the right values, can be a powerful force for good in the world.

God doesn't just want to meet us on Sunday mornings or when we are on our knees in prayer—He desires to be present in every aspect of our lives. Whether you are working in a factory, running a small business, or leading a vast enterprise, when you make decisions grounded in Judeo-Christian principles, you invite God's wisdom into every moment. This doesn't mean that Judeo-Christian principles and prayer alone will make you wealthy or successful. Rather, they provide the foundation for a truly rich life—a life marked by peace, purpose, and integrity. When you align your dreams with God's plan, doors will open that you never expected to. Success may or may not come in the form of financial abundance, but it will lead to a life of fulfillment, joy, and deep connection with both God and others. When you choose to walk in faith, making decisions rooted in integrity and love, the true measure of success is found not in material wealth but in the impact you leave behind—a legacy of faithfulness, service, and the knowledge that you have lived a life aligned with God's purpose for you.

Lessons Learned

FAITH IS THE FOUNDATION. David Green's story demonstrates that faith is more than just a personal belief—it is a powerful force that can shape every aspect of life, including business. By grounding his business in Christian principles, David built a company that reflects his values, proving that faith and commerce can coexist in powerful ways.

PRAYER IS NEVER A SUBSTITUTE FOR HARD WORK AND PERSEVERANCE. David's success didn't come overnight—it was the result of years of hard work, sacrifice, and perseverance. His story is a testament to the power of resilience and a reminder that great things are possible when we refuse to give up on our dreams.

GENEROSITY IS A CALLING. For David, financial success was never an end in itself, but a means to bless others. His commitment to giving back is a reminder that true success is measured not by what we accumulate but by how we use our blessings to lift others up. In the same way that Eddie Rickenbacker (back in chapter 13) saw the preservation of his life as a gift God gave him in order to enable him to bless others, David saw his skills in business as a means of grace for those around him.

Chapter 20

SMALL DECISIONS, SEISMIC SHIFTS

In my sophomore year of high school, I decided I needed a job. Mama was working impossible hours, pulling double shifts just to cover the basic necessities of life. For most of my childhood, we moved around frequently because we could never afford to stay in one place for long. I went to four different elementary schools in four years. Poverty tends to make people very transient.

"Mama," I said one evening at the dinner table, "I'm going to find a job so I can help out with the bills." I remember the distinct feeling that it was time to step up and stop being a kid. It was time to be more responsible.

"Father God," Mama prayed right there at the dinner table, "speak to Timmy and give him direction. Awaken his imagination with ideas. You are good. And we thank You for your help each and every day."

A few days later, I decided to walk to the local mall after

school. I didn't have any money to spend, but I liked going anyway. There was something about wandering through the shops and imagining what I might be able to buy someday. As soon as I stepped into the mall, I heard someone call my name.

"Tim! How are you?"

I turned to see Roger Yongue, a kid from school. He was a couple of years older than me. We weren't close, but I remembered him as someone who was always kind.

"I'm good," I replied, noticing the uniform he was wearing. Roger had just come out of the movie theater's foyer.

"Hey," he said, "any chance you're looking for a job?"

"Um, yes," I said, my heart skipping a beat. "I was just talking to my mom about getting one."

"Well," Roger said, smiling, "we need to hire someone. I'd be happy to put in a good word for you."

I was stunned. I couldn't have hidden my excitement if I'd tried. You have to understand—this wasn't just any job. To me, this was *the* job. When I was growing up, we didn't have money for luxuries like movies. I'd been to an actual movie theater only a handful of times in my life, and each visit was pure magic. For us, going to the movies was a rare treat, something we anticipated for months. The idea of working at a theater, surrounded by movies, was like a dream come true.

To my amazement, a few days later, I was offered the job. Let me tell you—working at the Northwoods Mall theater was one of the best jobs I've ever had. It wasn't just a job; it was an adventure. I got to see films like *An Officer and a Gentleman, Rocky II, Star Trek II, Return of the Jedi, Superman III*, and more—all for free! This was my personal golden age of film, my coming-of-age moment. It wasn't just about the movies; it was about discovering who I was and who I wanted to be.

Some of my happiest memories are of working with Roger in that theater. We had one massive screen with seven hundred seats, and each movie played for four to six months at a time. Roger and I would often work twelve-hour shifts, and his positivity was infectious. Roger lived in a single-wide trailer, and his family was probably just as poor as mine. But Roger was always smiling, always cracking jokes, and always radiating this inexplicable joy.

One day, I couldn't help but ask him, "How is it that you're always so happy?"

Roger grinned and said, "Because Jesus Christ is alive. And He's the Lord of my life."

Being the bonehead I was back then, I pushed back. "No, seriously," I said. "I want to know what's really going on. There's got to be something bigger than that."

"Nope!" Roger laughed. "It really is that simple."

At the time, I wasn't ready to hear it. I didn't ask Jesus into my heart until years later, but, looking back, I credit Roger for planting the seed of salvation. That one conversation, so simple yet so profound, stuck with me. It became a quiet echo in my heart, waiting for the right time to take root.

I share this story not just because it's a personal memory but because it reflects a universal truth. It's the small, seemingly insignificant moments—the decision to walk to the mall, the choice to say yes to an unexpected opportunity—that often define the trajectory of our lives. I didn't go to the mall looking for a job that day, but the dream of getting one was on my radar. When the door opened, I sprinted through it. That one decision led to a series of events that would shape my entire future.

Sometimes, opportunity doesn't come with fanfare or a flashing neon sign. It comes quietly, like Roger calling my name in a mall. But when you recognize it and say yes, those small moments can change everything.

As a young teenager working at the local movie theater, I often visited Chick-fil-A during breaks. John Moniz was the owner/operator of the Chick-fil-A in the mall. I have written and spoken often about the massive impact John Moniz had on my life. He saw something in me that I didn't see in myself. As time passed, John took me under his wing, teaching me the importance of hard work, conservative business principles, and personal responsibility. He showed me that my circumstances didn't define my future and that I could overcome any obstacle with determination and strategic thinking. His mentorship instilled in me the belief that I could rise above poverty and achieve great things, laying the groundwork for my future successes in business and public service. John Moniz's guidance transformed my outlook and set me on the path to becoming the person I am today.

I tell this story for two reasons. First, to demonstrate that change always starts small. Seismic shifts that transform culture rarely happen in a moment. Life's little choices, gradual shifts in perspective, and consistent actions create lasting impact. One of my favorite movie lines of all time came from the character Maximus in the movie *Gladiator*: "What we do in life echoes in eternity." My taking the job at the movie theater was a minor decision. John Moniz's mentorship might have seemed like a small gesture at the time, but it sparked a transformation in my life that continues to resonate. I believe that the choice you and I make today will echo in eternity.

Earlier, I wrote that we are in a profound cultural moment. We didn't simply arrive at porous borders, radical gender ideology, failing schools, rising crime rates, weakened national security, and eroded trust in institutions all at once. There has been a consistent erosion of our moral and cultural values. By making small choices to step away from the Judeo-Christian values that have defined us for generations, we have gradually shifted the direction of our nation.

Churches are emptier than they have ever been. Faith and traditional family values are openly mocked. This is because we have not fought for our beliefs with the same fervor with which others have fought to dismantle them. Each step away from these foundational principles, each micro-concession made, has contributed to the current state of our society. If we want to restore our nation's strength and integrity, we must recognize the power of these small, incremental changes and work diligently not just to reverse the course but to chart a new way forward. This means actively supporting our faith communities, advocating for strong family structures, and reclaiming the values that have historically made our nation strong.

The second reason I tell this story is because opportunity is one of the fundamental pillars defining our history and our present. Opportunity is the essence of America. It is the driving force behind our business innovations and commercial successes. Opportunity is the promise that anyone, regardless of their background, can achieve greatness through hard work and determination. It is the foundation upon which our nation was built, and it remains the beacon of hope for every American citizen striving for a better future.

As a young man, I had to walk a mile to find my opportunity. But I found it. Now I am doing everything in my power to make opportunity more readily available to every American, regardless of socioeconomic background. This mission to bring economic and educational opportunities to our hardest-hit communities consumes me. It keeps me up at night. Without a doubt, the achievement I am most proud of from my time in the Senate is the creation of Opportunity Zones.

With the help of President Donald Trump, we unleashed Opportunity Zones, which encourage investment in economically distressed communities. Over $84 billion in private sector dollars have been invested in these areas, providing new jobs, revitalizing neighborhoods, and offering hope where it was once in short supply. I have walked through countless neighborhoods transformed by these investments. Countless families have been lifted out of poverty because opportunity suddenly exists right outside their doors.

The positive impact of Opportunity Zones extends beyond mere economic improvement; they are rejuvenating the spirit of these communities. Children now have safer, more vibrant places to play. Local businesses are thriving, and the quality of education is improving as schools receive more support. This initiative is about more than just financial investment—it's about restoring dignity and creating a foundation for lasting success.

My commitment to this cause is unwavering. Seeing the tangible changes in these communities reaffirms my belief that any community can thrive with the right support and opportunities. This is not just a policy—it's a pathway to a brighter future for all Americans.

All of this stemmed from my wild imagination, my dreaming with God as I stared at the ceiling and dreamed of the movie *Rocky*. All of this is a testament to the power of faith, small decisions, and the relentless pursuit of opportunity.

The journey from a fourteen-year-old in search of a job to a U.S. Senator has been defined by faith and imagination. The small choices, the seemingly insignificant decisions, and the everyday acts of courage and hope have all woven together to create a life of purpose and impact.

Faith has been the cornerstone of this journey. Faith that my mother instilled in me at our dinner table, praying for guidance and inspiration. Faith that kept me going during long walks home in the dark, and opened my eyes to John Moniz's mentorship. Each step, guided by a belief in something greater, has reinforced the idea that we are all part of a larger story in which our small actions can have eternal echoes.

It is the small, everyday choices that define our lives. Most people dream of the big moments in life—promotions, engagements, having kids, going on vacation. These are beautiful milestones, to be sure, but they are not the primary ingredients for a successful life. The everyday acts, the small choices, and the consistent habits shift the course of a life. Nothing great will happen without discipline and consistent steps in the same direction. This is as true for an individual as it is for a nation.

Strong character is built through countless small decisions made with integrity. Waking up early to exercise, choosing to listen rather than speak, and showing kindness to a stranger are seemingly insignificant actions that accumulate to form a life of purpose and achievement. A successful life is not made in a day of grand gestures but in the quiet, steadfast commitment to doing the right thing, day in and day out.

For our nation, the principle is the same. The Founding Fathers laid a foundation based on enduring principles—faith, liberty, and justice. These ideals were not realized through a single act but through a series of small, consistent efforts and sacrifices.

If we are going to build a strong and prosperous nation, we must commit to small, everyday acts of citizenship and integrity. Voting in local elections, being kind to and helping our neighbors, speaking out at our school board meetings, and advocating for justice in our communities will steer the course of our country's future. Each of us has the power to influence our nation's future through our daily choices. It's about creating a legacy of integrity, discipline, and unwavering commitment to doing what is right.

Lessons Learned

SMALL DECISIONS CAN HAVE A LIFE-CHANGING IMPACT. As a fifteen-year-old, I decided to walk a mile to the mall in search of a job, a seemingly insignificant choice that ultimately shaped the direction of my entire life. Even the smallest decisions, fueled by determination and imagination, can open doors to opportunities that change the course of one's future.

MENTORSHIP AND GUIDANCE ARE CRUCIAL TO SUCCESS. My encounter with John Moniz at Chick-fil-A provided me with the mentorship I didn't know I needed. John saw potential in me and taught me essential life lessons about hard work and responsibility. I cannot overstate the importance of having a mentor to guide us and inspire us to realize our full potential!

FAITH AND IMAGINATION CAN LEAD TO UNEXPECTED OPPORTUNITIES. My ability to dream led me to a job at the movie theater that eventually connected me with John Moniz. Faith, coupled with imaginative thinking, can reveal possibilities that seem out of reach, helping us break through barriers.

Conclusion

NEW BEGINNINGS

A lot has changed in the world and in my life since I wrote the first words of this book. The most exciting news is that on August 3, 2024, I married the love of my life and became a bonus dad, all on the same day. While I always hoped I would one day marry, these things are often out of our control. I prayed for many years for the right woman to come along. And then, one day, there she was! Obviously, everything about my life changed with this decision to share my life with her.

Marriage is a profound reminder that life is constantly renewing itself, offering us opportunities to reflect, recalibrate, and move forward with purpose. New beginnings are about more than simply turning the page—they are about building on what came before while dreaming of what can be. They force us to acknowledge the past, with its triumphs and mistakes, and invite us to imagine the future in ways that align with our values.

New beginnings are priceless in life. New beginnings allow us to reestablish boundaries and redefine goals. New beginnings are God's reminder that He is always at work, even when we can't see it. They give us a chance to embrace hope, to write a new chapter in our story, and to trust in His perfect timing. This new chapter for me reminds me that we never truly finish growing, learning, or loving.

New beginnings are also an opportunity to reflect on where we've been while keeping our eyes fixed on where we're going. They challenge us to become better versions of ourselves—whether as a spouse, a parent, or a leader. And through it all, I believe that God's plan is always bigger and better than our own!

In many ways, my personal journey mirrors the broader journey of our nation. America, too, is at a moment of new beginnings, a crossroads where we need to remember where we came from while charting a path for where we want to go. But these new beginnings are not without their challenges. Whether in our personal life or in the life of this great nation, starting anew often requires a return to what is true, what is foundational. It requires us to go back to our roots, not out of nostalgia, but because those roots contain the values and principles that will sustain us.

For America, those roots are the Judeo-Christian values that have been the bedrock of every major institution since our founding. From the establishment of our legal system to the development of our educational frameworks, social services, and the human rights movements that have defined our nation's moral compass, these values have been our foundation. They extend beyond laws and policies—they are reflected in every aspect of our society. Whether in our agricultural practices or our disaster response efforts, these values are what compel us to care for our neighbors, to serve the common good, and to preserve the dignity of every individual. The belief in equality, justice, and liberty, grounded in faith, has guided America through its greatest triumphs and its most challenging times, providing the moral clarity to build a nation that seeks to uphold freedom and compassion for all.

The stories I've shared in this book reflect that truth. We've seen how the faith of ordinary men and women sparked an extraordinary change—how people like Horatio Spafford, whose personal tragedies could have easily broken him, instead found strength in faith to praise God in the storm. We've witnessed how dreamers like my grandmama Louida imagined a better future, even when faced with the harshest realities of her time. Her faith and resilience, passed down through generations, embody the strength that has always been at the heart of this nation.

These stories are not isolated examples; they are part of a larger, more profound narrative about who we are as a people. They remind us that faith is not just a private comfort—it is a public force for good, woven into the very fabric of our nation. These values are the threads that hold together the tapestry of America, shaping our culture, inspiring generations, and guiding us through our greatest challenges. From the abolition of slavery to the Civil Rights Movement, it was faith in action that moved mountains and brought justice to the oppressed. This legacy of faith-driven service is embedded in our institutions and our communities, reminding us that the strength of our nation lies in the moral convictions that guide us to serve one another and uphold the common good.

This book is more than a reflection on the past—my sincere hope is that it can be a road map for how to navigate the present and secure a better future. It is a call to return to the Judeo-Christian values that built this nation and to let those values once again inform every aspect of our lives: from our laws to our schools, from our families to our public discourse.

The task ahead may seem overwhelming, but we are not without hope. We are not without strength. We stand on the shoulders of those who came before us, and just as they overcame adversity through faith and determination, so too can we. The faith that guided them is the same faith that will guide us today if we are willing to reclaim it!

We must remember that though this work will not be easy, it is the work we are called to do. Our country will never be perfect, but it was meant to continuously strive toward a more perfect union, and that striving has always been fueled by a deep, abiding faith in God and in the principles He laid out for us. Those principles are as relevant today as they were when the Founders first put pen to paper and declared that our rights come not from man but from our Creator.

In the face of the challenges we now encounter—moral confusion, cultural division, and the erosion of foundational institutions—we must return to the values that have guided us through wars, economic downturns, and societal upheaval. These are not just abstract ideas; they are the guiding truths that have held this nation together for centuries, and they will continue to do so if we have the courage to live by them.

But let's not lose sight of the need for action! This book is a call to rise up in faith, to stand firm in our convictions, and to actively participate in the work of restoring our country. We must get on our knees in prayer, as so many of our ancestors did, and then rise to our feet with the resolve to act. The task may be great, but our God is greater, and with His guidance, no mountain is too high and no challenge too difficult.

As I enter this new phase of my own life, I am filled with hope for the future—both for my family and for this nation. I am reminded daily that faith is not passive. It is active, living, and powerful. And it is through that faith that we will find the strength to face the challenges ahead, just as those who came before us did.

The work ahead is immense, but so is the reward. We are building a legacy—not just for ourselves but for the generations to come. Just as the prayers of my grandmama and mama echoed through my life, shaping me into the man I am today, so too will our prayers and our actions echo through the lives of our children and grandchildren.

What we do today will echo in eternity. Let us make sure those echoes are ones of faith, hope, and unwavering commitment to the values that have always made America great.

ACKNOWLEDGMENTS

I have been blessed in more ways than I can count, but writing this book has once again reminded me of the people who have shaped my journey and supported me every step of the way. Reflecting on this, I am overwhelmed with gratitude and am incredibly grateful for the many friends, mentors, and loved ones who have left their mark on my life. While there are far too many to name, I want to acknowledge those whose stories have been woven into mine and who stood by me as I wrote this book.

First and foremost, to my incredible wife, Mindy: Your love, faith, and unwavering encouragement have been the greatest gifts of my life. I couldn't have walked this journey without you.

To my grandparents, Artis and Louida Ware: Your strength, love, and unshakable foundation have shaped me in ways beyond measure. To my mom, Frances Scott, and my aunt (Doretha) Nita Smith: Thank you for your endless support, your wisdom, and for always reminding me of the deep roots that shaped my faith and resilience. And to my nephew, Ben—heir to all the Scotts—who reminds me every single day: "The best is yet to come!"

To Roger Yongue, Joe McKeown, and Jennifer DeCasper: You have been by my side through every twist and turn of this journey. Your friendship, wisdom, and unwavering support mean more to me than words can express.

To my dad and stepmom, to Earl and his family, and to my dear friend Trey Gowdy: Your insight, encouragement, and steadfast friendship continue to inspire and challenge me daily. Thank you for walking this path with me. I am beyond grateful.

And finally, to Joel Clark, and to Eric Nelson, Hannah Long, and the entire team at HarperCollins: Your passion and dedication made this book possible. Thank you for your belief in this message and for your tireless work to bring it to life. I am truly grateful.

NOTES

1. "Communications: The Anti-Liberty Meeting in — —," *The Liberator* (Boston), October 24, 1835, 170. https://www.loc.gov/item/sn84031524/1835-10-24/ed-1/.
2. William Lloyd Garrison, *Selections from the Writings and Speeches of William Lloyd Garrison* (Boston, 1852), 378–87. https://tile.loc.gov/storage-services/public/gdcmassbookdig/selectionsfromwr00garr/selectionsfromwr00garr.pdf.
3. Ibid., 382–86.
4. Wendell Phillips Garrison and Francis Jackson Garrison, *William Lloyd Garrison, 1805–1879: The Story of His Life Told by His Children*, vol. 2 (New York, 1885), 26. https://archive.org/details/williamlloydgarr02ingarr/page/26/mode/2up?q=upset.
5. *Selections from the Writings and Speeches*, 389.
6. "Too Intensive Advertising Campaign Unveils Fake Freshman Boomed for Class Treasurer," *Daily Princetonian* 60, no. 155 (December 7, 1935).
7. Marissa Webb, "The Notorious Fictitious Ephraim di Kahble '39's Candy Wrapper Exhibit," *Princeton Alumni Weekly*, May 14, 2021. https://paw.princeton.edu/article/notorious-fictitious-ephraim-di-kahble-39s-candy-wrapper-exhibit.
8. "Ghost Army Veterans: Fred Fox," Ghost Army. Accessed March 3, 2025. https://ghostarmy.com/bio/f/Ghost_Army_Veterans/286/.
9. Rick Beyer, "Freddy Fox Goes to War," *Princeton Alumni Weekly*, January 21, 2016. https://paw.princeton.edu/article/freddy-fox-goes-war.
10. This scene is a dramatization.
11. Jonathan Gawne, *Ghosts of the ETO: American Tactical Deception Units in the European Theater 1944–1945* (Casemate, 2002), 286.
12. Jim Saksa, "After Decades of Secrecy and Years of Lobbying, Congress Grants Ghost Army Gold Medal," *Roll Call*, March 21, 2024. https://rollcall.com/2024/03/21/congress-grants-ghost-army-gold-medal/.
13. Joshua Skovlund, "World War II Ghost Army Veterans Receive the Congressional Gold Medal," *Task & Purpose*, March 21, 2024. https://

taskandpurpose.com/culture/ghost-army-veterans-congressional-gold-medal/.
14. Danny Thomas and Bill Davidson, *Make Room for Danny* (G. P. Putnam's Sons, 1991), 33–34.
15. Ibid., 76–81.
16. Ibid., 13–14.
17. Rufus King, *The Life and Correspondence of Rufus King*, ed. Charles King, vol. 3 (New York, 1806), 545. https://archive.org/details/rufuskinglife03kingrich/page/545/mode/1up.
18. Chris Fenner, "It Is Well with My Soul," Hymnology Archive, July 5, 2018. https://www.hymnologyarchive.com/it-is-well-with-my-soul.
19. Ibid.
20. George William Pilcher, *Samuel Davies: Apostle of Dissent in Colonial Virginia* (University of Tennessee Press, 1971), 4–5.
21. Ibid, 7.
22. Thomas Kidd, "The Great Awakening in Virginia," *Encyclopedia Virginia*, last updated December 7, 2020. https://encyclopediavirginia.org/entries/great-awakening-in-virginia-the/.
23. Samuel Davies, "Memoir of President Davies," *Quarterly Register* IX, no. 4 (May 1837): 4. https://static1.squarespace.com/static/590be125ff7c502a07752a5b/t/64300cc78cee486ac1d48119/1680870600159/.Davies%2C+Samuel%2C+Memoir+of+President+Davies+%281837%29.pdf.
24. William Bland Whitley, "Samuel Davies (1723–1761)," *Encyclopedia Virginia*. Last updated December 22, 2021. https://encyclopediavirginia.org/entries/davies-samuel-1723-1761/.
25. Bronzeman, "Biographical Sketch of Samuel Davies," February 28, 2015. https://thebridgeonline.net/biographical-sketch-of-samuel-davies/.
26. Ben C. Dunson, "Samuel Davies, Colonial Presbyterian Patriot," *American Reformer*, July 19, 2024. https://americanreformer.org/2024/07/samuel-davies-colonial-presbyterian-patriot/#fnref-11604-1.
27. Thomas S. Kidd, *The Great Awakening* (Yale University Press, 2007), 290.
28. David Gollaher, *Voice for the Mad: The Life of Dorothea Dix* (Free Press, 1995), 18–23.
29. Francis Tiffany, *Life of Dorothea Lynde Dix*" (Boston, 1890), 21. https://archive.org/details/lifeofdorothealy00tiffuoft/page/20/mode/2up?view=theater.
30. Ibid., 2.
31. *Voice for the Mad*, 8–12, 4–7.
32. Ibid., 24.
33. Ibid., 26, 8.
34. Ibid., 27–28.
35. *Life of Dorothea*, 25–26.
36. *Voice for the Mad*, 92, 110–13.
37. *Life of Dorothea*, 334–35.
38. Helen Brown, "Apollo 13 Had a Near-Zero Chance of Survival—but Mum Always Thought Dad Would Make It Back," *Telegraph*, August 25, 2024. https://www.telegraph.co.uk/films/2024/08/25/apollo-13-survival-netflix-nasa-jim-lovell/.

39. John O'Leary, host, *Live Inspired*, podcast, season 9, episode 90, "Apollo 13 Spacecraft Commander Jim Lovell," July 12, 2018. Relevant portion at 37:27 timestamp. https://open.spotify.com/episode/4O5jX6HK46Dow8Netve5xz?si=a7c08a9d88b44041.
40. James A. Lovell Jr., interview by Ron Stone, May 25, 1999, transcript, NASA Johnson Space Center Oral History Project, JSC History Collection, University of Houston—Clear Lake, Houston, TX. https://historycollection.jsc.nasa.gov/JSCHistoryPortal/history/oral_histories/LovellJA/LovellJA_5-25-99.htm.
41. NASA, "Apollo 13: Mission Details," Nasa.gov, July 8, 2009. https://www.nasa.gov/missions/apollo/apollo-13-mission-details/.
42. Brown, "Apollo 13."
43. Lovell, NASA Johnson.
44. "When I looked back and saw that tiny Earth, it snapped my world view," Anders said. "Here we are, on kind of a physically inconsequential planet, going around a not particularly significant star, going around a galaxy of billions of stars that's not a particularly significant galaxy—in a universe where there's billions and billions of galaxies. Are we really that special? I don't think so." Quoted in Ron Judd, "With a View from Beyond the Moon, an Astronaut Talks Religion, Politics and Possibility," *Seattle Times*, December 7, 2012. https://www.seattletimes.com/pacific-nw-magazine/with-a-view-from-beyond-the-moon-an-astronaut-talks-religion-politics-and-possibilities/.
45. Lovell, NASA Johnson.
46. Jim Lovell and Jeffrey Kluger, *Lost Moon: The Perilous Voyage of Apollo 13* (Houghton Mifflin, 1994), 135.
47. Jo Ann Zuñiga, "NASA Flight Director Says Faith, Family Have Marked His Life's Journey," *Crux*, August 2, 2019. https://cruxnow.com/church-in-the-usa/2019/08/nasa-flight-director-says-faith-family-have-marked-his-lifes-journey.
48. Erin Blakemore, "Buzz Aldrin Took Holy Communion on the Moon. NASA Kept It Quiet," History, July 17, 2024. https://www.history.com/news/buzz-aldrin-communion-apollo-11-nasa.
49. "Joshua Glover," National Parks Service. https://www.nps.gov/people/joshua-glover.htm.
50. "Great Excitement at Racine!" *Daily Sentinel*, March 11, 1854. http://www.wishistory.com/mar11.html.
51. Ruby West Jackson, *Finding Freedom: The Untold Story of Joshua Glover, Runaway Slave* (Wisconsin Historical Society Press, 2007), 49. https://books.google.com/books?id=7t-QnYX19DAC&lpg=PP1&pg=PR4#v=onepage&q&f=false.
52. Joel Winters, "Joshua Glover: A Refugee of the 1850's," Etobicoke Historical Society. https://www.etobicokehistorical.com/joshua-glover.html.
53. "Guideposts Classics: Eddie Rickenbacker on Helping Others," *Guideposts*. https://guideposts.org/prayer/power-of-prayer/guideposts-classics-eddie-rickenbacker-on-helping-others/.
54. Eddie Rickenbacker, *Rickenbacker* (Prentice-Hall International, 1967), 296.
55. Ibid., 308.

56. "John Bartek's Speech about the Rickenbacker Rescue," Auburn University, November 19, 1998. https://www.lib.auburn.edu/archive/find-aid/528/speech.htm.
57. *Rickenbacker*, 317.
58. Ibid., 329.
59. Ibid., 344.
60. Charles C. Mann, *The Wizard and the Prophet: Two Remarkable Scientists and Their Daring Visions to Shape Tomorrow's World* (Knopf, 2018), 181, EPUB.
61. Ibid., 189.
62. While inspired by various accounts of Norman Borlaug's childhood, these scenes are dramatizations.
63. Mann, *Wizard and the Prophet*, 130.
64. Ibid., 154.
65. Norman Borlaug, "The Green Revolution, Peace, and Humanity," Nobel Lecture, December 11, 1970, Oslo, Norway. https://www.nobelprize.org/prizes/peace/1970/borlaug/lecture/.
66. Jason H. Gart, "He Shall Direct Thy Paths: The Early Life of George W. Carver," National Park Service: Midwest Regional Office, 2014, 48. https://npshistory.com/publications/gwca/hrs.pdf.
67. Christina Vella, *George Washington Carver: A Life* (Louisiana State University Press, 2015), 15–16.
68. Gart, "He Shall Direct," 79.
69. Ibid., 50.
70. Ibid., 44.
71. "Making the Flag," Smithsonian National Museum of American History. Accessed January 29, 2025. https://amhistory.si.edu/starspangledbanner/making-the-flag.aspx.
72. This story is inspired by contemporary accounts but is a dramatization that condenses events.
73. David Green, "Investing in Others Through God's Love," interview by Jim Daly, *Focus on the Family with Jim Daly*, podcast, July 28, 2017. https://www.focusonthefamily.com/episodes/broadcast/investing-in-others-through-gods-love/.
74. David Green and Bill High, *Giving It All Away . . . and Getting It All Back Again: The Way of Living Generously* (Zondervan, 2017), 41.
75. "Hobby Lobby Stores," *Forbes Profile*. Updated November 2024. https://www.forbes.com/companies/hobby-lobby-stores.

ABOUT THE AUTHOR

Senator Tim Scott is a champion of opportunity, faith, and the American Dream. Raised in poverty by a single mother who worked long hours as a nurse's assistant, Tim nearly failed out of high school before a mentor's wisdom—and his mother's unwavering faith—helped him turn his life around.

Now, as the longest-serving Black senator in U.S. history and the only Black lawmaker to ever serve in both the House and Senate, Tim fights every day to expand economic mobility, improve education, and empower hardworking families. A lifelong optimist, he believes America's best days are still ahead.

Tim was serving on the Charleston County Council before he built a successful small business. He later served in the South Carolina State House and the U.S. House of Representatives before joining the Senate in 2013. Reelected in 2022, he currently serves as the chairman of the Senate Committee on Banking, Housing, and Urban Affairs.

Driven by faith and purpose, Tim is on a mission to uplift a billion people with the message of hope and opportunity—because if he could rise from poverty to the U.S. Senate, he knows others can, too.